SAMMY
DOG DETECTIVE

SAMMY
DOG DETECTIVE

BY

Colleen Stanley Bare

SCHOLASTIC INC.

New York Toronto London Auckland Sydney
Mexico City New Delhi Hong Kong

To Andy

ACKNOWLEDGMENTS

The author wishes to thank police officer Andy Schlenker for his invaluable assistance with this project, and also to acknowledge the helpful support of his wife, Anita, and children, Nick and Gene. The cooperation of the Modesto, California, City Police Department K-9 Unit under the supervision of Sgt. Gene Balentine is also greatly appreciated.

ISBN 0-439-15982-2

12 11 10 9 8 7 6 5 4 3 2 1   0 1 2 3 4 5/0

Printed in the U.S.A.   24

First Scholastic printing, February 2000

Designed by Charlotte Staub

Sammy is like most pet dogs.
He is lovable, huggable, friendly,
and tries to steal kisses.

He is also different from most pet dogs,
because Sammy is a dog detective.
He works for a police department
eight hours a day,
five days a week.

Sammy is the canine part of a K-9 team.
The other half is a police officer named Andy.
The two work together to protect people
and property. They also live together,
because Sammy is Andy's family dog.

Both of Sammy's parents were working
police dogs. His K-9 mother was a German
Shepherd, the breed most often used in police
work. His K-9 father was a Belgian Malinois,
known for its intelligence and speed.
Sammy has the best traits of both.
He is smart, strong, fast,
loyal, and brave.

STAY AWAY
POLICE DOG

The team of Andy and Sammy does many jobs.
When Andy commands, the dog searches areas,
buildings, and cars. Just the sight of big,
barking Sammy scares most criminals.
They usually put up their hands and shout,
"Don't let him bite me. I give up!"
Sammy also helps Andy find
missing persons and
control crowds.

How did Sammy learn to be a police dog?
He couldn't read about it in a book,

HOW TO BE
A GOOD
POLICE
DOG

or on a computer.

Instead, Sammy went to K-9
school, starting at age one year.
He trained almost every day.
At eighteen months, he was the
youngest dog ever to pass
the K-9 tests in his
police department.

Sammy's first training was in **obedience**.
He was taught to heel, or to go to Andy's
left side — and to come, stay, sit,
lie down, and bark.
He also learned hand signals for each.
They are used when Sammy is too far away
to hear or if quiet is needed.

HEEL

SIT

LIE DOWN

BARK

Next came lessons in agility, search, and attack.
These are skills that he often needs at work.
Agility training involves jumping and
climbing, which Sammy
really enjoys.
He climbs ladders and over barrels and walls.
He jumps hurdles and through open windows.
He walks on narrow planks above the ground
and crawls through tunnels.

Search training uses Sammy's super sense
of smell. When Andy says "track," the dog puts
his nose to the ground and starts sniffing.
To locate hidden objects out-of-doors, such as a
gun or knife, he hunts for any articles that smell
different to him. When he finds one, he barks.
Not only does he sniff out weapons, he also may
bark at a comb, shoe, bottle cap, piece of paper,
anything unusual in that setting.

Sometimes Sammy is ordered to find a person
hiding inside one of several large wooden
boxes. Sammy sniffs each box until he
detects the human. Then he barks
until Andy summons him.

When Andy and Sammy hunt for someone
inside a building, Andy gives Sammy
the command "search." The dog runs
through the building, sniffing, until
he discovers the suspect. Sammy
barks until Andy calls him back.
The dog has been trained to "bark instead of
bite" and never to bite unless Andy tells him
to do so. Although Sammy has assisted in at
least one hundred arrests, he has only had
to bite twice. Each time the "bad guy"
was running away. One was a burglar.
The other had hit a policeman.

Attack training is difficult for some dogs, but not
for brave Sammy. When a trainer wearing a
padded sleeve waves a club at Sammy,
Andy says "get him!" Sammy leaps at
the trainer's protected arm, grabs it
with his teeth, and holds on. He
only lets go when Andy says
"out," meaning "let go."
Sammy's ability to attack on command could
save Andy's life or his own some day.

Fireworks are used to teach Sammy to ignore
loud sounds such as gunfire. He also learns
to enter buildings filled with smoke,
created by using smoke bombs.

These lessons are repeated over and over.
When Sammy makes a mistake, patient
Andy never hits him. He just says
"no!" and shows disapproval.
He rewards Sammy's good behavior by saying
"good boy" — and with a hug, a pat,
and often a treat.

Sammy trains for several hours each week
and for a full day once a month.
He gets extra practice by entering many police
K-9 contests. He competes with up to
sixty dogs in obedience, agility,
search, and attack.

Sammy has won trophies in every K-9 trial he has ever entered. He is ranked as "Number One" police dog in the Western States Police Canine Association.

Sammy leads two lives. He is a tough dog detective, working for the police. And he is a beloved pet, living at home with his family. He does almost everything that the family does. At night, he sleeps on Andy's or the children's beds, causing crowding.

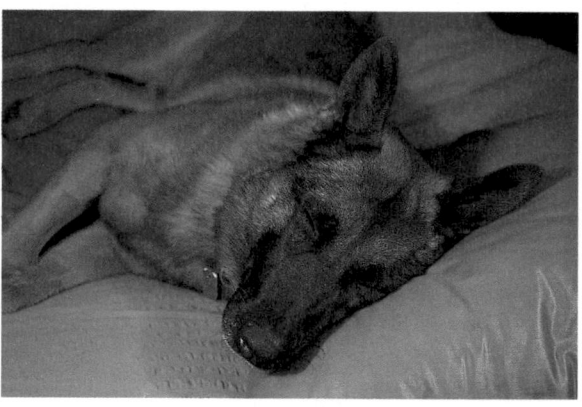

In the morning, Sammy brings in the sometimes slobbery newspaper.

He has
frequent
baths,

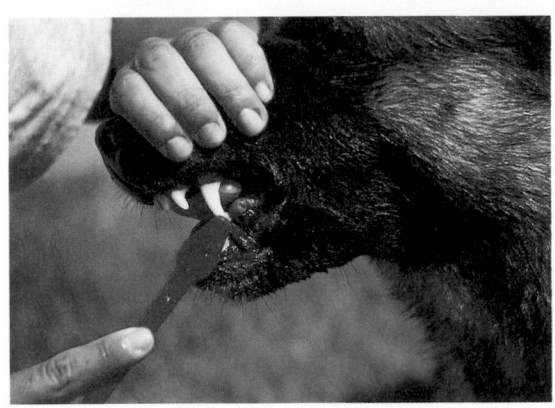

and gets
his teeth
brushed.

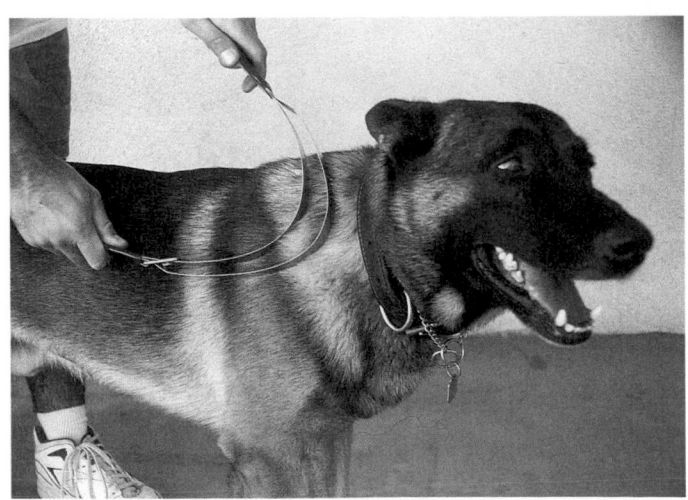

His coat is
groomed with
a special
tool.

Sammy plays ball and swims
with the children.

Sammy shares in family
picnics, vacations, and celebrations.
At Christmas, he has his own presents.
His favorite is a rawhide bone.

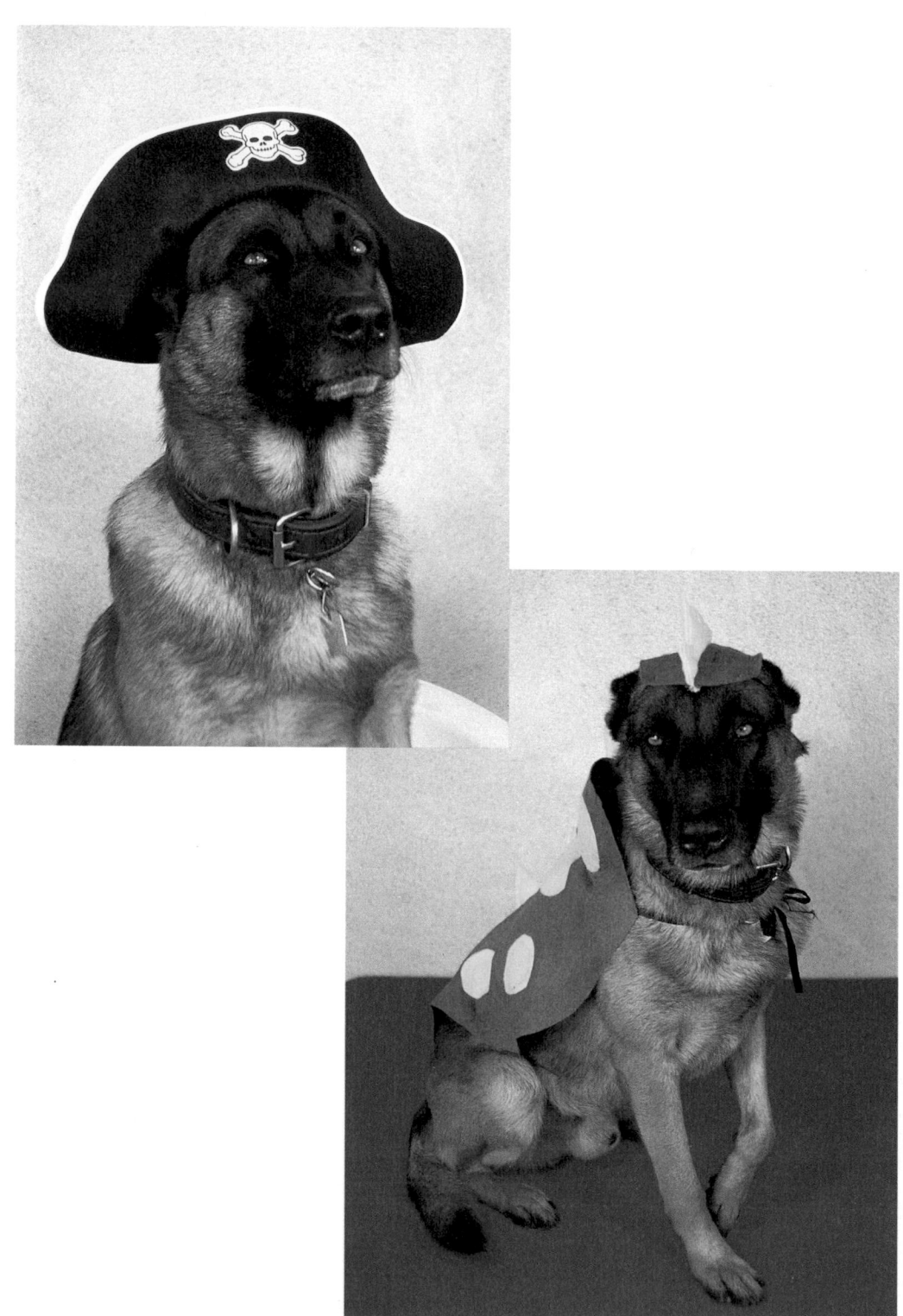

Sammy goes trick-or-treating on Halloween.
The children put hats on him.
One year he was a dinosaur.

Another year he was a pirate.

Children love Sammy, and Sammy
loves children.

Andy and Sammy give K-9 programs at schools.
The students laugh when Sammy jumps
in and out of a police car window.

Everyone wants to pat Sammy.

He reaches for kisses.

Sammy loves being a police dog.
On his days off, when he can't go to work,
he gets bored and sometimes howls.

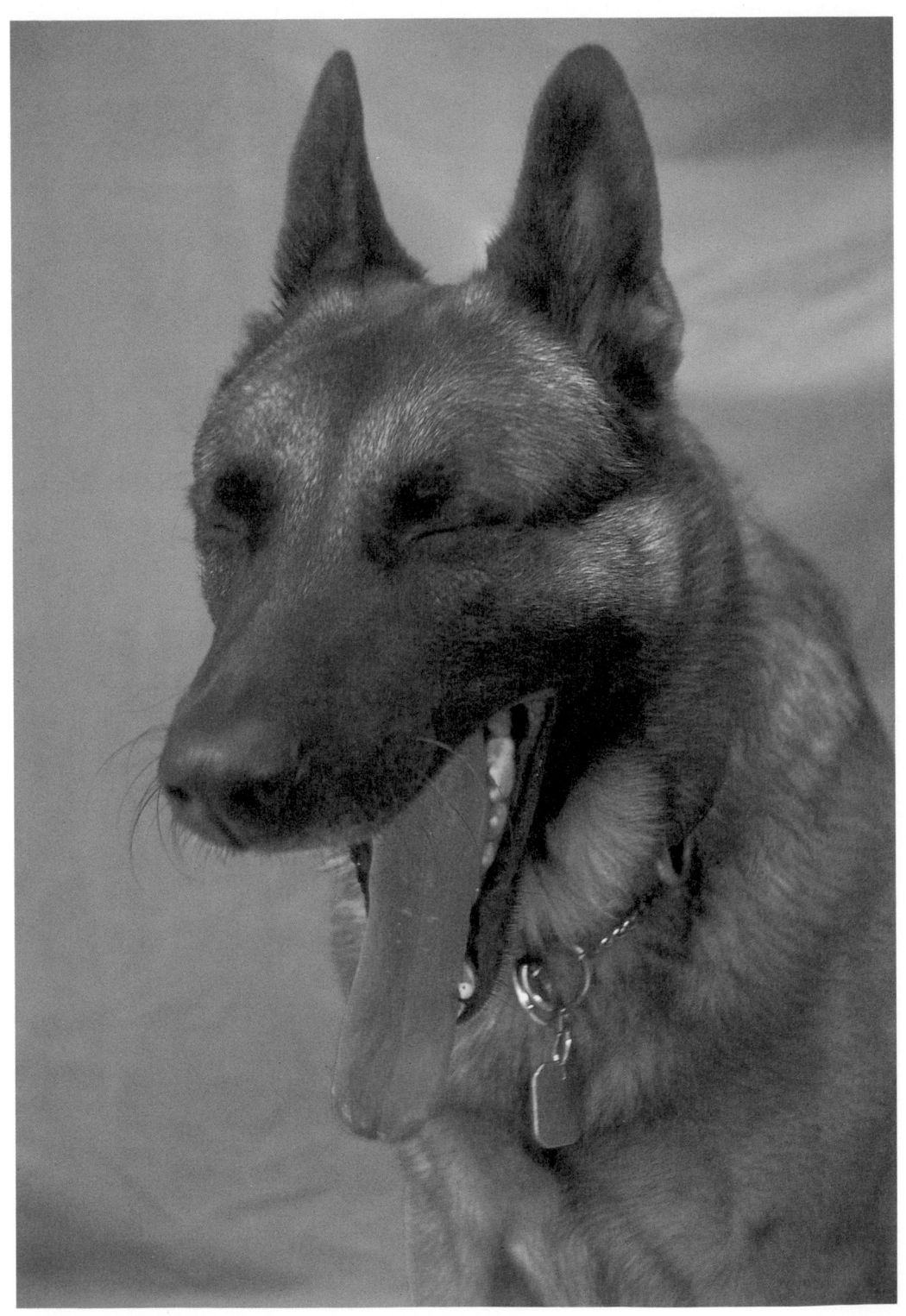

Sammy and Andy are close friends.
They are a team, working together to make
their world a safer place.

INDEX

EX MACH[INA]

RING OUT THE OLD

CREDITS

BRIAN K. VAUGHAN: WRITER
TONY HARRIS: PENCILS
JIM CLARK & TONY HARRIS: INKS
JOHN PAUL LEON: ART (GREEN)

THANKS TO GARTH ENNIS, JIM LEE & RICHARD FRIEND FOR THEIR CONTRIBUTIONS TO ISSUE #40

JD METTLER: COLORS
JARED K. FLETCHER: LETTERS

Ex Machina created by Vaughan and Harris
Cover by Harris & Mettler
Original series covers by Harris
Variant Cover to Green by John Paul Leon and Jonny Rench

...en Abernathy	Editor, Original Series
...risty Quinn	Assistant Editor, Original Series
...risty Quinn	Editor
...arry Berry	Art Director
...iane Nelson	President
...an DiDio and Jim Lee	Co-Publishers
...eoff Johns	Chief Creative Officer
...ohn Rood	Executive Vice President–Sales, Marketing and Business Development
...atrick Caldon	Executive Vice President–Finance and Administration
...my Genkins	Senior VP–Business and Legal Affairs
...teve Rotterdam	Senior VP–Sales and Marketing
...ohn Cunningham	VP–Marketing
...erri Cunningham	VP–Managing Editor
...lison Gill	VP–Manufacturing
...avid Hyde	VP–Publicity
...ank Kanalz	VP–General Manager, WildStorm
...ue Pohja	VP–Book Trade Sales
...lysse Soll	VP–Advertising and Custom Publishing
...ob Wayne	VP–Sales
...ark Chiarello	Art Director

EX MACHINA: RING OUT THE OLD. Published by WildStorm Productions, an imprint of DC Comics. 888 Prospect St. #240, La Jolla, CA 92037. Cover and compilation Copyright © 2010 Brian K. Vaughan and Tony Harris. All Rights Reserved. EX MACHINA is ™ Brian K. Vaughan and Tony Harris. Originally published in single magazine form as EX MACHINA #40-44 © 2009 and EX MACHINA SPECIAL #4 © 2009 Brian K. Vaughan and Tony Harris.

WildStorm and logo are trademarks of DC Comics. The stories, characters, and incidents mentioned in this magazine are entirely fictional. Printed on recyclable paper. WildStorm does not read or accept unsolicited submissions of ideas, stories or artwork. PRINTED IN USA. Second Printing.

DC Comics, a Warner Bros. Entertainment Company.

ISBN: 978-1-4012-2694-7

Chapter 1

Ruthless

WHAT THE HELL, MAN?

WEDNESDAY, OCTOBER 6, 2004

WRITERS.

NO RESPECT FOR DEADLINES...

RIGHT. WELL. I GUESS YOU PROBABLY WANNA SWING BY YOUR HOTEL AND CHANGE FIRST?

NAH, I'M COOL.

YOU'RE WEARING THAT? TO *CITY HALL?*

WE'RE INTERVIEWING FOR A JOB, NOT GETTING GAY MARRIED.

NO, I KNOW...BUT IT COULD BE AN *AMAZING* JOB, RIGHT?

DOING THE MAYOR'S BIOGRAPHY AS A COMIC BOOK? HOW COOL IS IT THAT HE'S GIVING SOMETHING BACK TO THE MEDIUM HE GREW UP LOVING?

EVERYBODY NEEDS A GIMMICK.

NATHAN HALE

ABERNATHY SAYS MELTZER AND HITCH ARE AT THE TOP OF THE SHORTLIST, BUT I THINK WE MIGHT ACTUALLY STAND A CHANCE.

I MEAN, WE'RE UNDERDOGS, BUT SO WAS HUNDRED GOING INTO THE ELECTION, RIGHT? MAYBE HE'LL *IDENTIFY* WITH US.

IS THAT CRAZY?

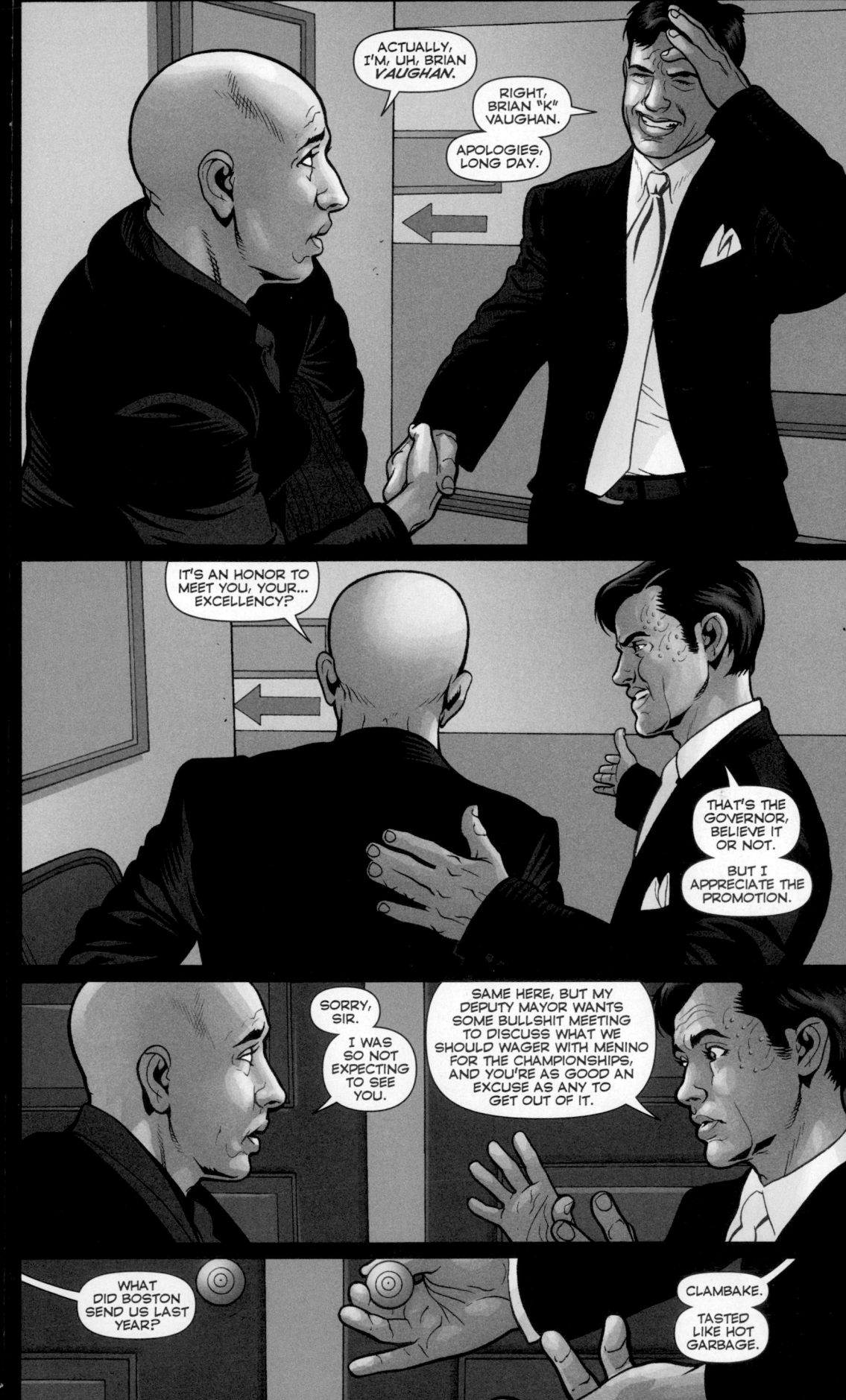

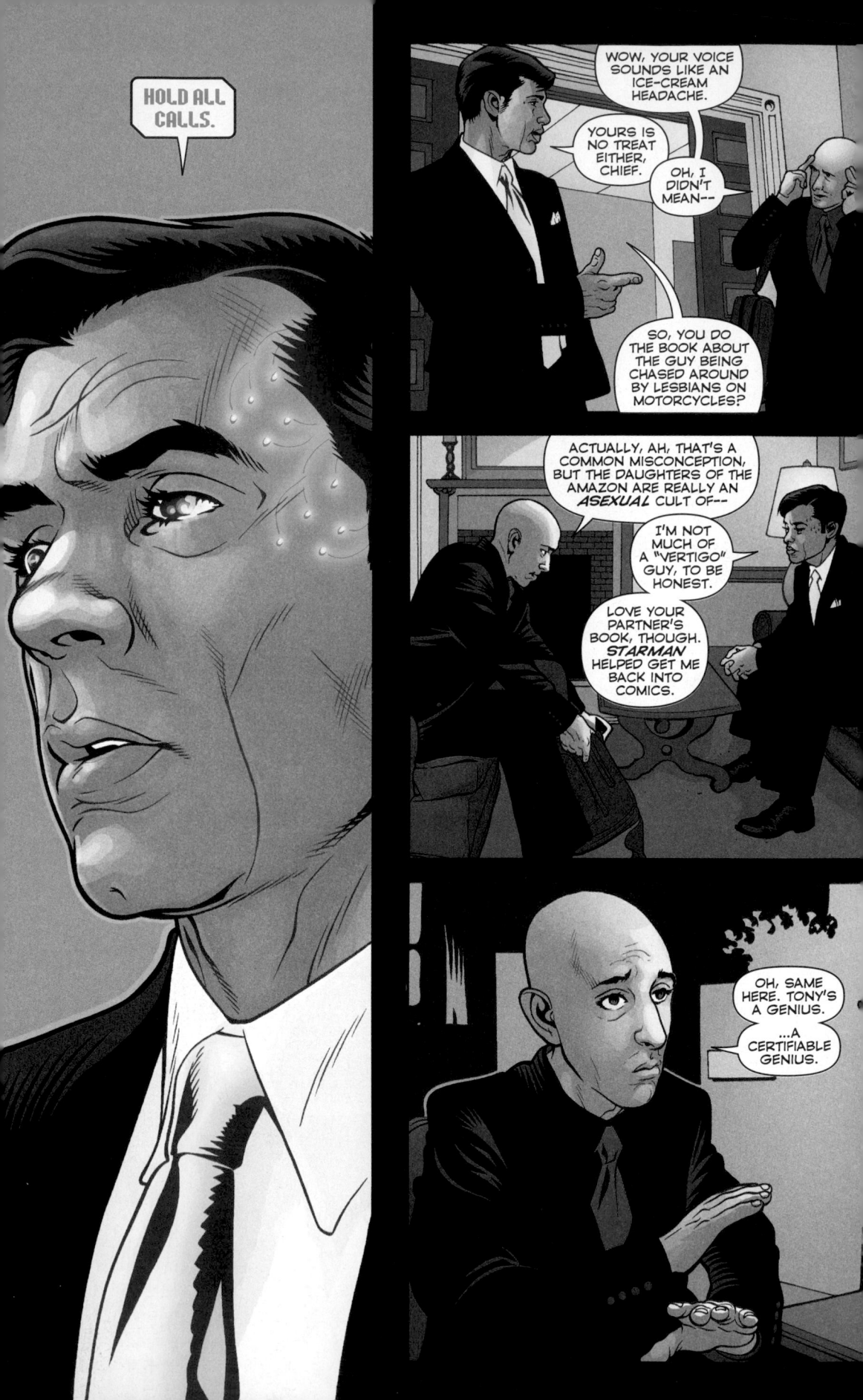

THIS IS *MY* CITY!

LOVE IT OR LEAVE IT...IN A *BODY BAG!*

GRRRAARRRGHH!

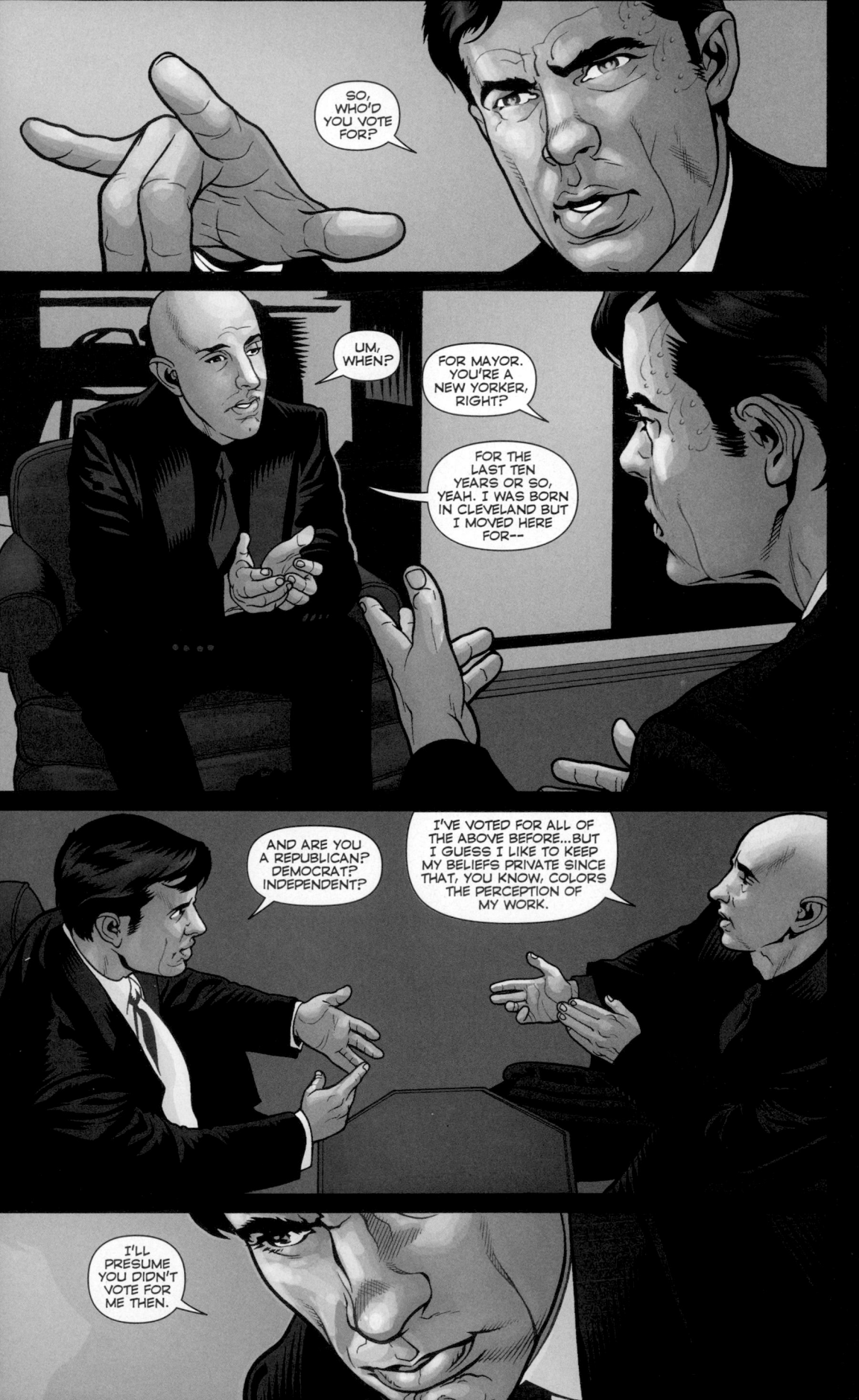

SIR...

NO, I APPRECIATE THE HONESTY.

WHEN LEVITZ CORNERED ME AT A FUNDRAISER ABOUT DOING A GRAPHIC NOVEL FOR CHARITY, I TOLD HIM TO SEND ME HIS WHOLE PAYROLL, REGARD- LESS OF THEIR "LEANINGS."

SPEAKING OF WHICH, ARE YOU SEEING ANYBODY?

DO YOU MEAN... AM I DATING SOMEONE?

I'M MAKING SMALL TALK, BRIAN, NOT HITTING ON YOU.

YEAH. A GIRL. KIND OF, I MEAN.

SHE'S KIND OF A GIRL?

NO! NO, SHE'S ALL WOMAN. BUT WE'RE...KINDA DATING. IT'S A LONG-DISTANCE THING. SHE MOVED TO CALIFORNIA LAST YEAR. FOR GRAD SCHOOL.

AND WHY THE HELL DIDN'T YOU FOLLOW HER?

BECAUSE OF YOU.

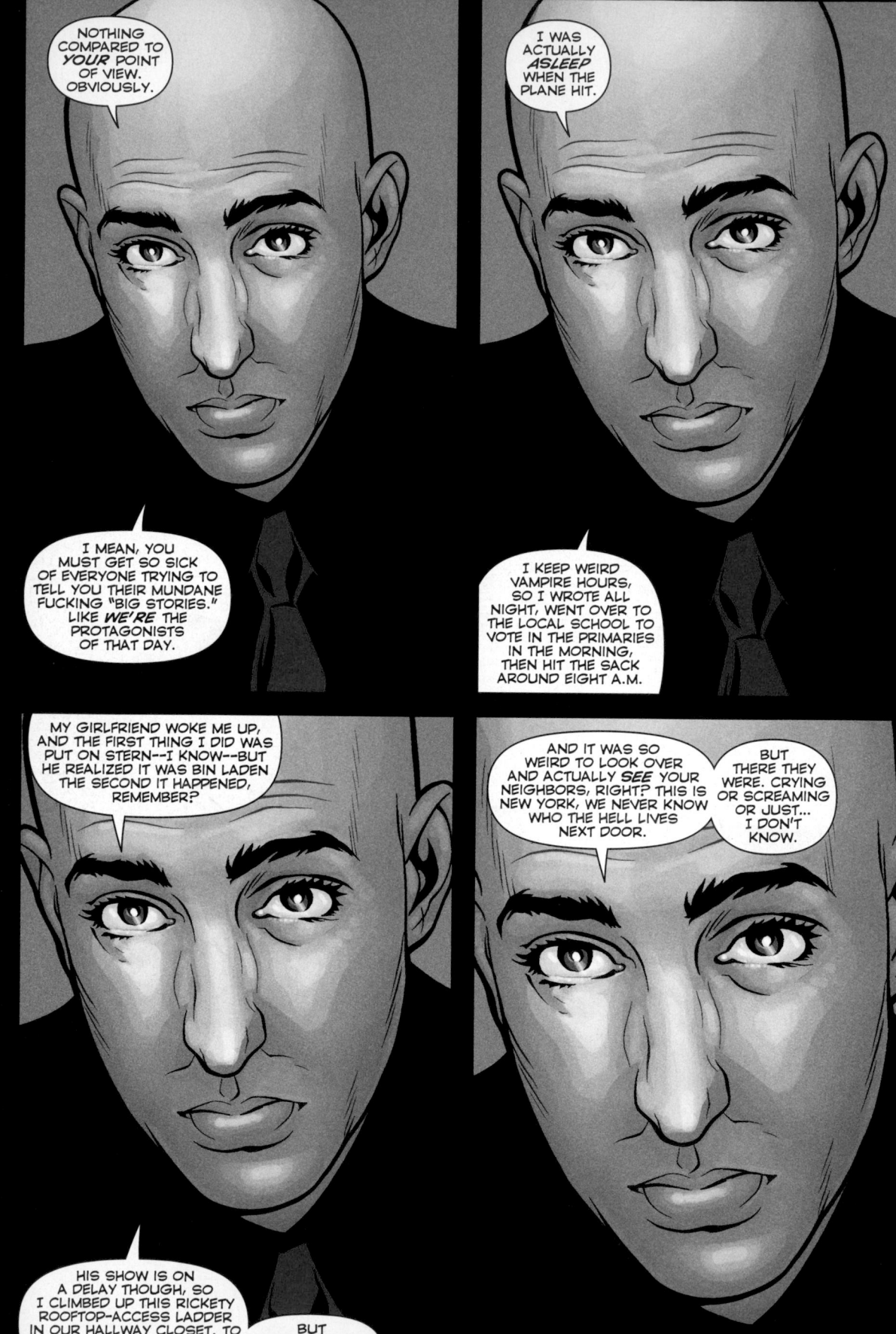

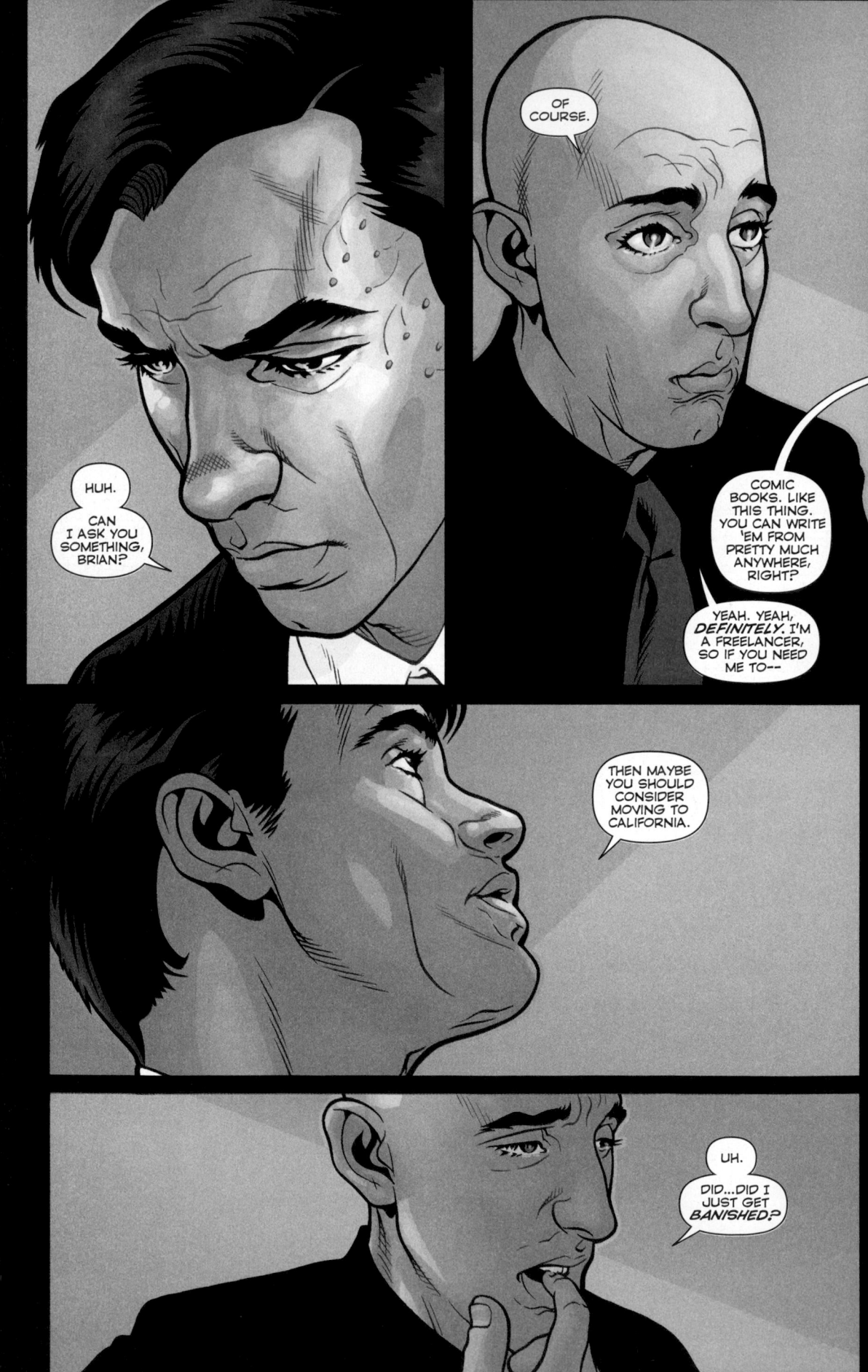

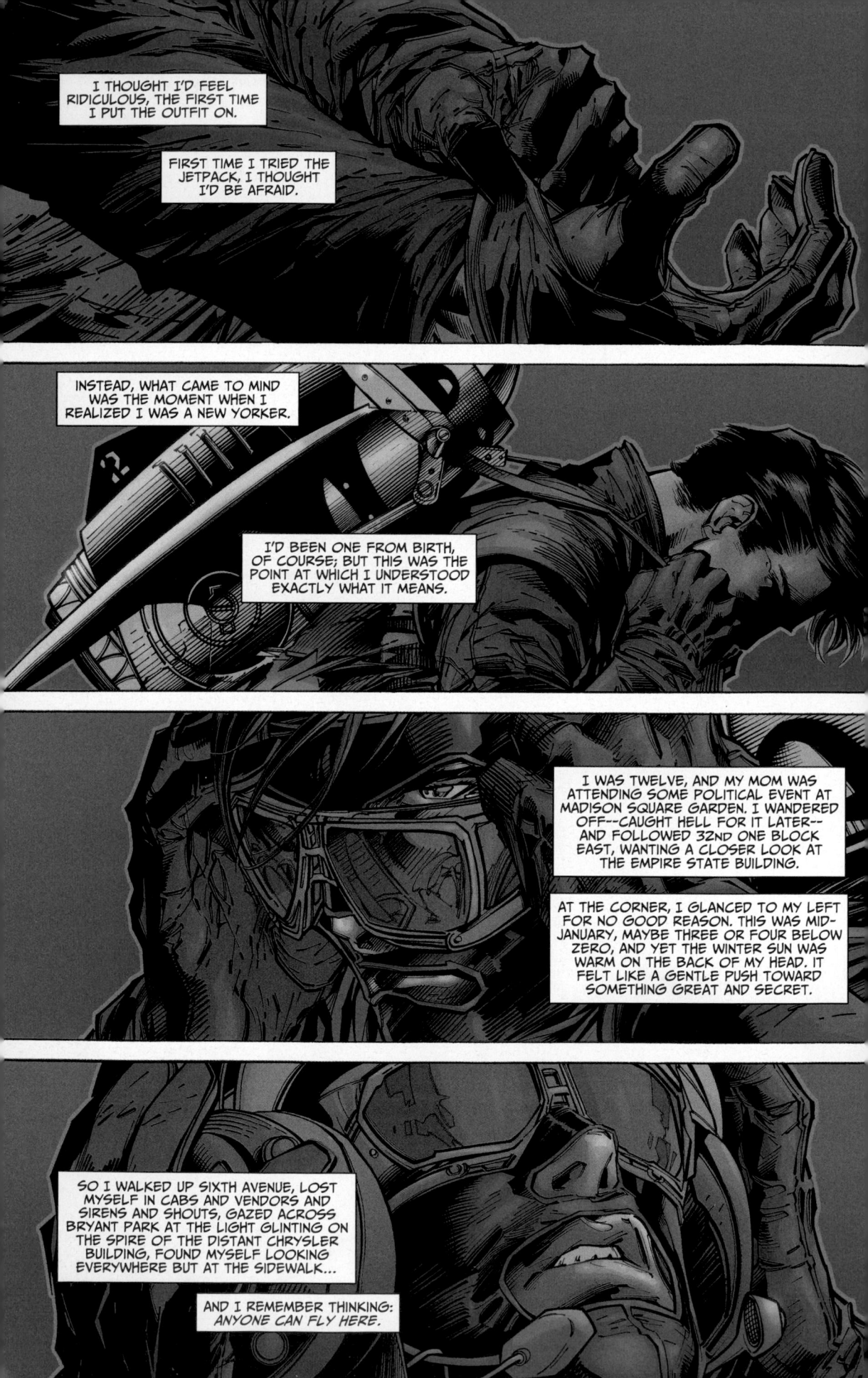

I THOUGHT I'D FEEL RIDICULOUS, THE FIRST TIME I PUT THE OUTFIT ON.

FIRST TIME I TRIED THE JETPACK, I THOUGHT I'D BE AFRAID.

INSTEAD, WHAT CAME TO MIND WAS THE MOMENT WHEN I REALIZED I WAS A NEW YORKER.

I'D BEEN ONE FROM BIRTH, OF COURSE; BUT THIS WAS THE POINT AT WHICH I UNDERSTOOD EXACTLY WHAT IT MEANS.

I WAS TWELVE, AND MY MOM WAS ATTENDING SOME POLITICAL EVENT AT MADISON SQUARE GARDEN. I WANDERED OFF--CAUGHT HELL FOR IT LATER-- AND FOLLOWED 32ND ONE BLOCK EAST, WANTING A CLOSER LOOK AT THE EMPIRE STATE BUILDING.

AT THE CORNER, I GLANCED TO MY LEFT FOR NO GOOD REASON. THIS WAS MID-JANUARY, MAYBE THREE OR FOUR BELOW ZERO, AND YET THE WINTER SUN WAS WARM ON THE BACK OF MY HEAD. IT FELT LIKE A GENTLE PUSH TOWARD SOMETHING GREAT AND SECRET.

SO I WALKED UP SIXTH AVENUE, LOST MYSELF IN CABS AND VENDORS AND SIRENS AND SHOUTS, GAZED ACROSS BRYANT PARK AT THE LIGHT GLINTING ON THE SPIRE OF THE DISTANT CHRYSLER BUILDING, FOUND MYSELF LOOKING EVERYWHERE BUT AT THE SIDEWALK...

AND I REMEMBER THINKING: *ANYONE CAN FLY HERE.*

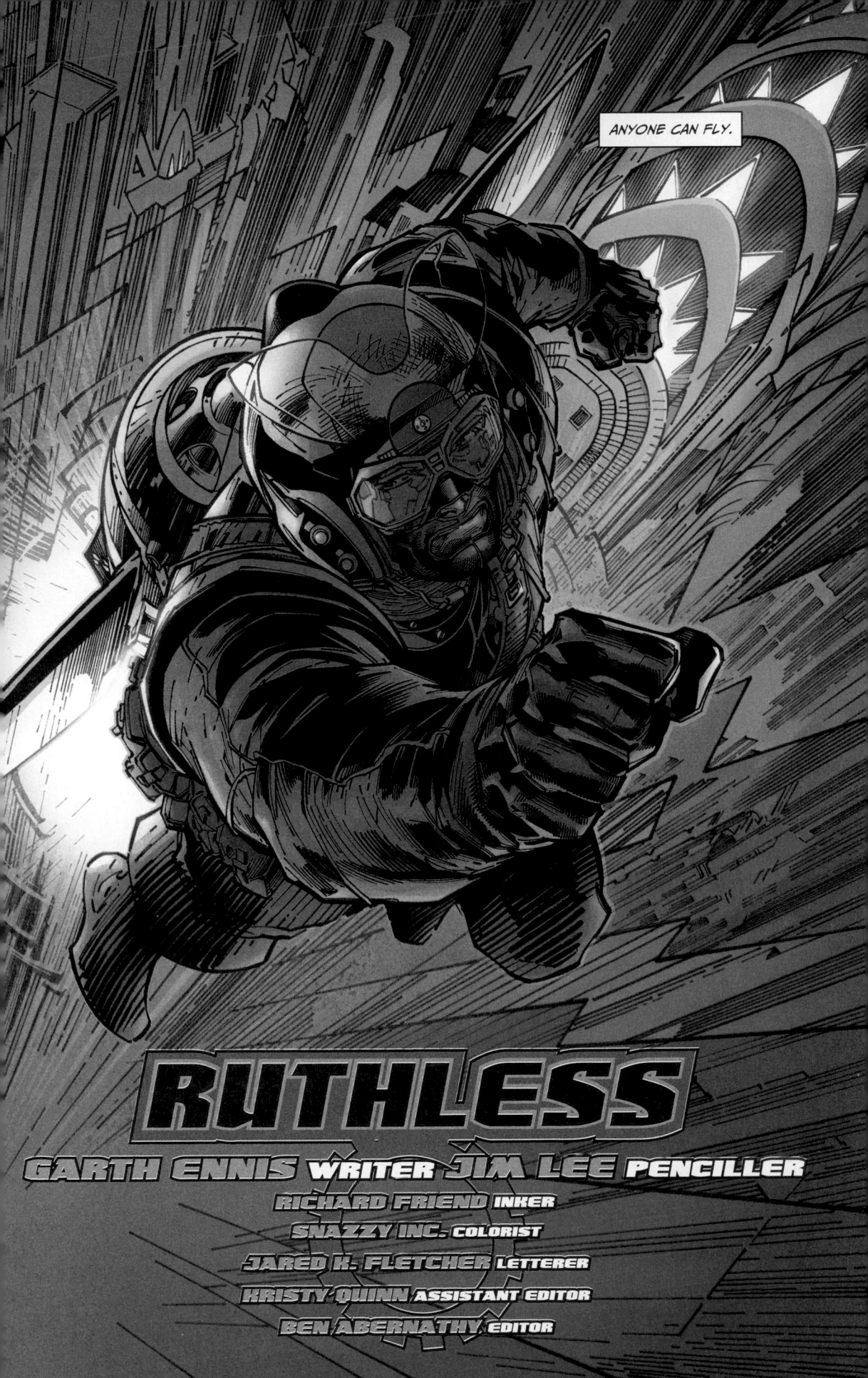

Green

Chapter 2

EVER SINCE LAST YEAR'S BLACKOUT, I'VE BEEN LOOKING FOR NEW WAYS TO MAKE US LESS DEPENDENT ON THIS COUNTRY'S--FORGIVE ME--PIECE OF CRAP POWER GRID.

BUT AS A FORMER CIVIL ENGINEER, I REALIZED THAT NONE OF THE EMERGING NEXT-GEN ALTERNATIVES WERE ANYWHERE CLOSE TO BEING COMMERCIALLY VIABLE, WHICH IS WHEN I STARTED LOOKING TO THE *PAST*.

WITH SOME FINANCIAL ASSISTANCE FROM MY EVER-GRACIOUS FORMER OPPONENT MIKE BLOOMBERG, I WANT TO BRING REAL RENEWABLE ENERGY TO TOWN.

I WANT OUR POWER TO BE CHEAP AND I WANT IT TO BE CLEAN, AND THAT MEANS ADDING *WIND TURBINES* TO EVERY BRIDGE AND SKYSCRAPER THAT CAN SUPPORT THEM.

IF UGLY-ASS OLD WOODEN WATER TOWERS COULD BECOME AN ICONIC PART OF OUR TWENTIETH-CENTURY SKYLINE, THERE'S NO REASON THAT THESE SLEEK, BEAUTIFUL MACHINES CAN'T BE THE TOUCHSTONES OF THE TWENTY-FIRST.

SO...OFF YOUR STUNNED SILENCE, I GUESS I'LL TURN IT OVER TO MY DIRECTOR OF LONG-TERM PLANNING AND SUSTAINABILITY FOR YOUR QUESTIONS.

FIRST ONE OF YOU TO MAKE A CRACK ABOUT *ME* SUPPLYING ALL THE HOT AIR FOR THIS PROJECT GETS THEIR PRESS CREDENTIALS REVOKED.

YEAH, I THOUGHT SO.

AND NO ONE WAS TELLING YOU WHAT TO WRITE, JUST WHAT *NOT* TO POLLUTE OUR LANDFILLS WITH.

HOW IS THAT YOUR PLACE? MY PAPER IS A GORGEOUS, GRAPHICS-HEAVY PUBLICATION, NOT BIRDCAGE LINER LIKE THE *POST.*

BESIDES, DO YOU HAVE ANY IDEA HOW MUCH RECYCLED PAPER *COSTS?* WHO ARE YOU TO FORCE A PRIVATE COMPANY TO BUY A MORE EXPENSIVE PRODUCT?

EVERY OTHER MAJOR PAPER IN TOWN HAS FOUND A WAY TO DO IT.

MAYBE THAT'S WHY THEIR CIRCULATIONS ARE ALL GOING DOWN THE TOILET WHILE *OURS* IS GOING THROUGH THE ROOF.

CLEAN WHITE PAPER FOR A CLEAN WHITE READERSHIP, HUH?

THAT'S NOT FAIR.

NEITHER ARE YOUR EDITORIALS.

SEE YOU IN THE FUNNY PAGES, ED.

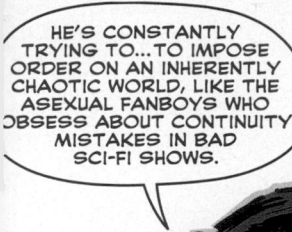

HE'S CONSTANTLY TRYING TO...TO IMPOSE ORDER ON AN INHERENTLY CHAOTIC WORLD, LIKE THE ASEXUAL FANBOYS WHO OBSESS ABOUT CONTINUITY MISTAKES IN BAD SCI-FI SHOWS.

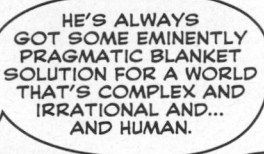

HE'S ALWAYS GOT SOME EMINENTLY PRAGMATIC BLANKET SOLUTION FOR A WORLD THAT'S COMPLEX AND IRRATIONAL AND... AND HUMAN.

YEAH, YEAH, THE GEEK SHALL INHERIT THE BLAH, BLAH, BLAH.

KERRACK

THE HELL?

JUST GRAB THE PHONE IN CASE THERE'S REALLY...

SOMEONE'S ON YOUR BALCONY.

EDDY, I'M NINE STORIES UP.

YOU THINK THE BIG BAD MAYOR PUT HIS *JETPACK* BACK ON SO HE COULD FLY UP HERE AND SCARE YOU?

I CAME TO SEE YOU.

HEY, BOSS.

YOU HEAR WHAT'S BLACK AND WHITE AND RED ALL OVER?

ANY CHANCE THIS CAN WAIT, RIDDLER? THE SANITATION COMMISSIONER'S BEEN ON HOLD SINCE LABOR DAY.

THAT NEWSPAPER DOUCHE, GUY WHO PUBLISHES THE *SOUND*?

HE GOT *MURDERED* LAST NIGHT.

JESUS CHRIST, ARE YOU SERIOUS? I WAS JUST TALKING TO HIM YESTERDAY!

AFRAID IT'S NOT ALL GOOD NEWS.

THE PSYCHO WHO OFFED HIM SAYS *YOU* TOLD HIM TO DO IT.

WHAT?

DON'T WORRY, THIS IS ALL FROM MY GUY INSIDE THE DEPARTMENT.

IT HASN'T HIT THE STREET YET.

BRADBURY, IF *YOU* KNOW ABOUT IT, IT'S ONLY A MATTER OF TIME BEFORE THE PRESS HEARS THAT I'M SUPPOSEDLY HIRING PEOPLE TO *ASSASSINATE* MY DETRACTORS.

WELL, *THAT'D* MAKE 'EM THINK TWICE BEFORE PUBLISHING BAD SHIT ABOUT YOU.

THIS ISN'T FUNNY.

YOU'VE GOT TO TAKE ME OVER TO HOMICIDE OR... OR WHOEVER THE HELL'S HOLDING THIS GUY.

SIR, YOU GOT NOTHING TO PROVE HERE.

YOU DIDN'T HIRE THIS NUT TO WHACK ANYBODY.

DID YOU?

JUST PUT THE BARREL DOWN, ALL RIGHT?

YOU GOT IT.

SplOsh

BIG MISTAKE, CHIEF.

I'VE GOT YOU ON DIGITAL VIDEO ILLEGALLY DISPOSING OF WASTE IN A PUBLIC--

UHNF!

UHN!

WHAT IS *WRONG* WITH YOU? I THINK I SPRAINED MY--

RAAAAAH!!

PANIC!

HUNF!

AHH! WHAT THE FUCK ARE YOU *DOING?!*

WARNING!
WARNING!

FOR FUCK'S SAKE...

HA HA!

WHY WASN'T I VIDEOTAPING *THAT!*

UM. GLIDE?

KERRASH

YOU'RE... NOT HERE TO LOOK FOR *CANNABIS*?

SIR, I CAN BARELY HANDLE *LITTERERS*, SO I'M GONNA HAVE TO WORK MY WAY UP TO DRUG DEALERS.

WAIT, YOU'RE THE *SUPERHERO* WHO STOPPED THAT SPEEDING TRAIN!

SOMETHING LIKE THAT.

LOOK, I DON'T CARRY MUCH CASH IN MY BELT, BUT...

YOU WANNA PAY ME BACK FOR THE ROOF, JUST KEEP ON TAKING CARE OF *MOTHER EARTH.*

RIGHT. ヨUHNE ANYWAY. I SHOULD PROBABLY CALL MY...SOMEBODY TO PICK ME UP.

SORRY I BLED ON YOUR PLANTS.

NO WORRIES, MAN.

IT'S THE OLDEST FERTILIZER OF THEM ALL.

EW, YOU *ATE* MY *BLOOD?*

NO, MY *PLANTS* DID. AND I ATE THEM.

AND THAT'S WHEN THE EARTH SHARED YOUR GIFT WITH ME.

CAMERA, BACK TO WORK.

SO WHAT, NOW YOU THINK YOU CAN TALK TO *TREES?*

IT'S MORE THAT *THEY* CAN TALK TO *ME.* EVEN AFTER DEATH, WOOD PULP CAN STILL SEND MESSAGES, YOU KNOW. THROUGH THE *NEWSPAPER.*

AND THE FALLEN FORESTS ALWAYS CHOOSE TO SPEAK TO ME THROUGH IMAGES OF *YOU.* THAT'S HOW I KNEW YOU WANTED THAT PUBLISHER DESTROYED.

WOW, HOWEVER LONG YOU'VE BEEN PRACTICING THAT LAME INSANITY DEFENSE, IT'S NOT ENOUGH.

YOU'RE JUST AN EXTREMIST ASSHOLE LOOKING FOR WHATEVER BULLSHIT COVER STORY WILL LET YOU OFF THE HOOK FOR YOUR LITTLE ACT OF "ECO-TERROR."

YOU TOLD ME TO KILL THE COMIC-BOOK PEOPLE NEXT.

WHAT DID YOU SAY?

THEY'RE THE WORST OFFENDERS OF THEM ALL. AT LEAST NEWSPAPERS ARE *EVENTUALLY* RECYCLED.

BUT COMICS ARE VIRGIN PAPER GOING INTO VIRGIN HANDS THAT TUCK THEM AWAY INTO POISONOUS PLASTIC. *FOREVER.* THOSE WHO CREATE AND CONSUME THEM WILL BE NEXT TO DIE.

LISTEN, GENIUS, YOU'RE ABOUT TO SPEND THE REST OF YOUR LIFE GETTING GANG-RAPED IN UPSTATE CORRECTIONAL.

YOU'RE NEVER GONNA HURT ANOTHER FUCKING SOUL.

OH, I'M NOT ALONE.

I'VE BEEN SELLING THE FOOD YOU BLESSED AT *FARMERS' MARKETS* ACROSS THE CITY.

THERE'S AN ENTIRE MOVEMENT OUT THERE NOW, JUST AWAITING YOUR INSTRUCTIONS.

THERE ARE NO GODDAMN INSTRUCTIONS!

EDWARD ROMANS
"He Spoke Truth to Power"

I'LL GIVE HIM THIS.

HE WAS A *BALLSY* GADFLY.

PRETTY DECENT LAY, TOO.

GET OUT.

IT WAS A MILLION YEARS AGO.

YOU'RE NOT THE ONLY ONE WITH A SHADOWY PAST.

SORRY, TOO MUCH INFORMATION?

IT'S NOT YOU.

I CAN'T STOP THINKING ABOUT WHAT THE SCUMBAG WHO KILLED HIM SAID...

WHO, MR. GREENJEANS?

SIR, HE'S A PARANOID SCHIZOPHRENIC WHO WENT OFF HIS MEDS THREE YEARS AGO. EVEN YOUR PALS IN THE NSA SAY HE DIDN'T HAVE ANY OF YOUR... *WHATEVER* IN HIS SYSTEM.

NOT THAT, ACTUALLY. IT'S WHAT HE SAID ABOUT *COMICS*.

COME AGAIN?

GUY WAS A BASKETCASE, BUT HE WASN'T WRONG THAT I'VE GIVEN A FREE PASS TO ALL THE *PERIODICALS* PUBLISHED IN THIS TOWN. WHY SHOULD NEWSPAPERS BE THE ONLY ONES ASKED TO SACRIFICE?

I MEAN, I HAVE SOME PULL WITH THAT COMMUNITY. I COULD PERSUADE THEM TO SWITCH TO POST-CONSUMER STOCK... AND SOMETHING CERTIFIED BY THE FOREST STEWARDSHIP COUNCIL, NOT THE LOGGING INDUSTRY'S SHILLS.

NO OFFENSE, SIR, BUT WHY WASTE ANYTHING ON SOMETHING THAT RINKY-DINK WHEN WE'RE GOING TO NEED EVERY LAST DROP OF POLITICAL CAPITAL TO GET YOUR TURBINES UP AND RUNNING?

YEAH, I KNOW. BUT WHAT IF ROMANS WAS *RIGHT?* WHAT IF THE WINDMILLS ARE JUST ANOTHER ADOLESCENT POWER FANTASY?

MAYBE THERE'S SOMETHING MORE *PRACTICAL* I COULD FOCUS ON.

WELL, YOU KNOW WHERE BOB DYLAN SAID ALL THE ANSWERS WERE, RIGHT?

BESIDES, PAPER IS YESTERDAY'S NEWS.

Ring Out the Old
part 1

Chapter 3

TUESDAY, MARCH 27, 2001

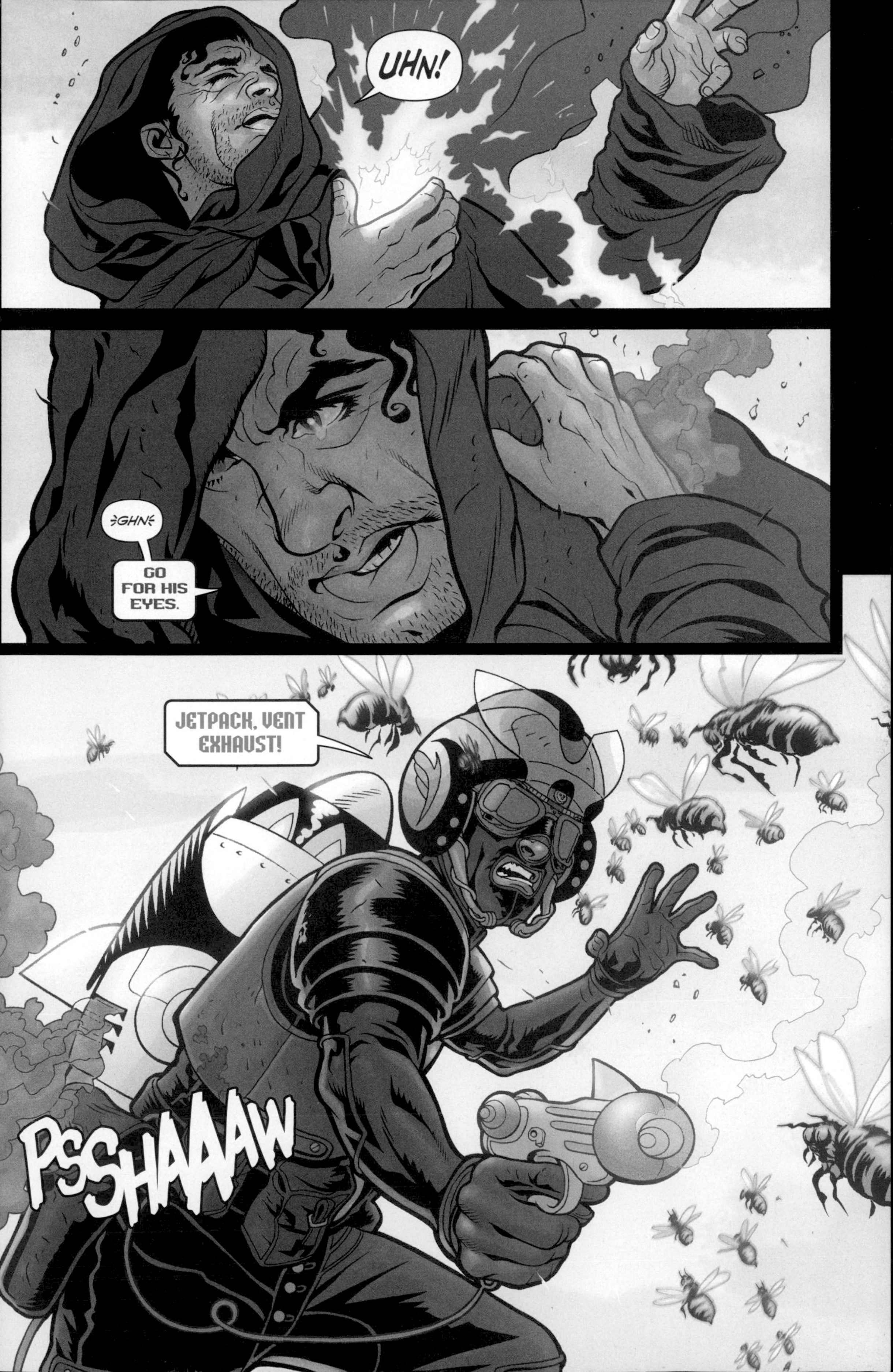
UHN!
GHN
GO FOR HIS EYES.
JETPACK, VENT EXHAUST!
PSSHAAAW

AND SO, CUTTING TO THE CHASE, I WILL *NOT* BE SEEKING A SECOND TERM AS YOUR MAYOR OF NEW YORK CITY.

WEDNESDAY, DECEMBER 29, 2004

MAYOR HUNDRED!

OVER HERE!

MAYOR HUNDRED!

MAYOR HUNDRED!

SIR!

MR. MAYOR!

I'M GUESSING THERE MAY BE QUESTIONS?

MAYOR HUNDRED!

IN THE BACK!

MAYOR HUNDRED!

I WAS FIRST!

MR. MAYOR, ARE THE RUMORS TRUE THAT WHATEVER GAVE YOU YOUR ABILITIES IS NOW *KILLING* YOU?

WHAT? GOD. NO.

AS ALWAYS, I'M HAPPY TO RELEASE WHATEVER PORTIONS OF MY MEDICAL RECORDS THE NSA WILL ALLOW ME TO SHARE, BUT THAT'S NOT WHAT THIS IS ABOUT.

BUT YOUR APPROVAL RATINGS ARE THE HIGHEST SINCE 9/11. IF YOU DECIDED TO RUN AGAIN--

IF I DECIDED TO RUN AGAIN, I'D SPEND EVERY MINUTE OF THE NEXT YEAR CAMPAIGNING, AND THE CITY CAN'T AFFORD SUCH A COLOSSAL WASTE OF TIME.

FOR ALL THE GOOD WE'VE ACCOMPLISHED, WE CONTINUE TO DIG OURSELVES DEEPER INTO A CRIPPLING DEFICIT, AND OUR SCHOOL SYSTEM IS STILL, FRANKLY, A CATASTROPHE.

SO HOW DO YOU FIX THEM BOTH IN JUST TWELVE MONTHS?

BY RAISING TAXES.

LIKE, A *LOT.*

I'LL BE INCREASING PROPERTY TAXES TWENTY PERCENT, UPPING THE CIGARETTE TAX NEARLY TWO DOLLARS, AND I'M AFRAID YOU'LL HAVE TO START THROWING A QUARTER INTO METERS ON SUNDAYS.

MORE IMPORTANTLY, A SURCHARGE WILL NOW BE APPLIED TO ALL INCOMES EXCEEDING $200,000, WITH THE LOCAL TOP MARGINAL RATE BEING SET AT SIXTEEN PERCENT.

SIR, WON'T SOME SUCCESSFUL NEW YORKERS VIEW THIS AS BEING *PUNISHED* FOR THEIR HARD WORK?

"IT IS NOT VERY UNREASONABLE THAT THE RICH SHOULD CONTRIBUTE TO THE PUBLIC EXPENSE, NOT ONLY IN PROPORTION TO THEIR REVENUE, BUT SOMETHING *MORE* THAN IN THAT PROPORTION."

THAT'S NOT KARL MARX, IT'S *ADAM SMITH*, THE FATHER OF CAPITALISM, A SYSTEM I HAPPEN TO FIRMLY BELIEVE IN...NO MATTER WHAT WILLIAM KRISTOL MAY WRITE ABOUT ME.

SO YOU AGREE WITH THOSE ON THE LEFT WHO SAY THAT PAYING TAXES IS OUR PATRIOTIC DUTY?

NO, I'M SAYING TAXES ARE A NECESSARY EVIL, WITH SLIGHTLY MORE EMPHASIS ON THE NECESSARY PART.

LOOK, OUR CITY IS IN REAL DANGER, AND WE'RE NOT GONNA BE ABLE TO SAVE IT BY *SHOPPING*.

AND WHAT IF YOU FAIL?

HOW ARE VOTERS SUPPOSED TO HOLD YOU ACCOUNTABLE IF YOU'VE ALREADY PLANNED YOUR *ESCAPE?*

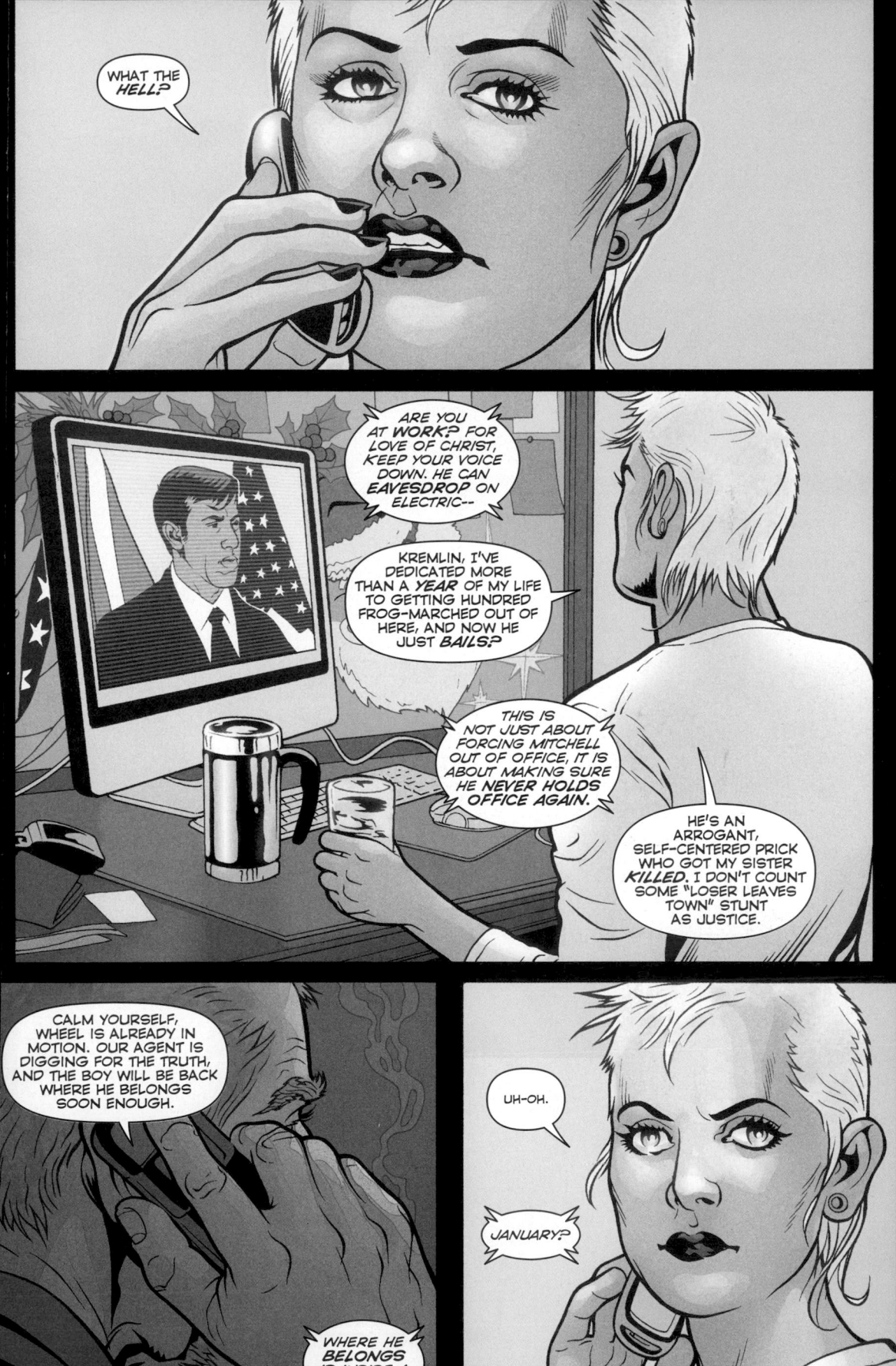

JOURNAL'S OLD JOB?

YOU'VE EARNED IT, JAN. AND I'M GONNA NEED ALL THE HELP I CAN GET FROM PEOPLE I TRUST.

AT LEAST HALF OF CITY COUNCIL WANTS MY HEAD FOR ESSENTIALLY BLOWING ANY SHOT AT THEM EXTENDING THEIR OWN TERM LIMITS.

YEAH, I, UH, KNOW YOU HAVE A LOT OF ENEMIES.

I WISH.

THESE DAYS, I JUST HAVE *OPPONENTS*.

THERE'S A DIFFERENCE?

YEAH.

ENEMIES STAB YOU IN THE FRONT.

≥HNF≤

≥HNF≤

HELP!

SHUT UP AND SPREAD, BITCH!

SOMEBODY HELP ME!

...

LADY. I HAVE NO IDEA WHAT YOU'RE TALKING ABOUT.

AND I GOT NOTHING ELSE TO SAY TO YOU!

NO WORRIES, MR. BRADBURY.

THAT WAS ALL THE CONFIRMATION I NEEDED.

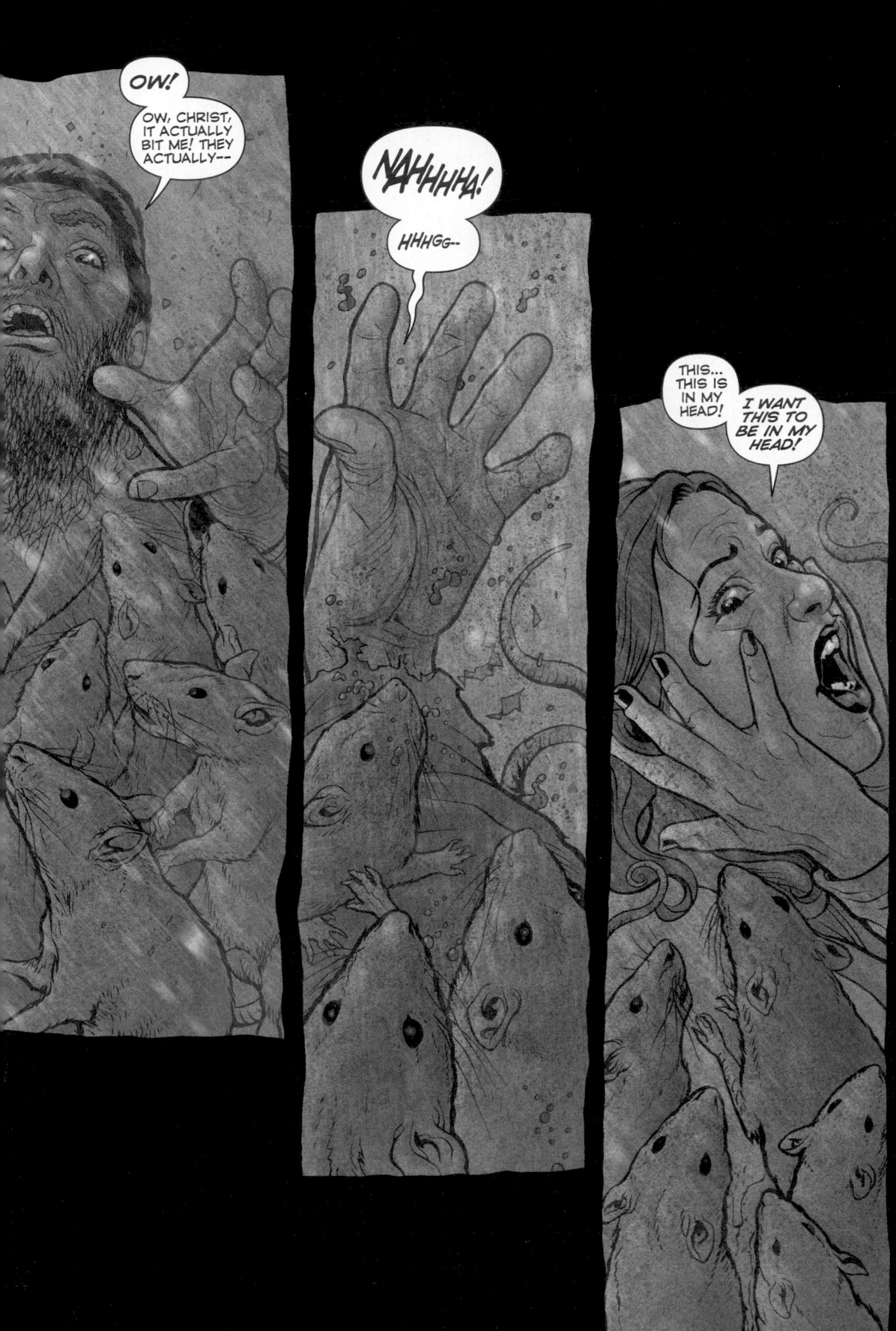

Ring Out the Old
part 2

Chapter
4

RAAARRRR

FRIDAY, MARCH 29, 2001

IT'S ALL RIGHT, GIRL.

THEY WON'T HURT YOU ANYMORE.

LONG TIME NO SEE, KID.

THURSDAY, DECEMBER 30, 2004

TRIP.

I DIDN'T THINK YOU WERE ALLOWED TO LEAVE ALBANY WITHOUT ADULT SUPERVISION.

CRAZED WIN...
Shuts down S...
for ELEVEN HO...

EASY, MR. MAYOR. THE GOVERNOR JUST WANTED ME TO OFFER YOU HIS *CONGRATULATIONS* ON YOUR VERY BRAVE PUBLIC ADDRESS YESTERDAY.

YOU ARE MY *SAVIOR.*

THOUGHT I'D BE TRAPPED DOWN THERE FOREVER WITH A GUY WHO SMELLS LIKE BALL SWEAT AND *RACKETEERING!*

BOSS, I'M SORRY. THAT REPORTER FROM THE *VOICE* TRACKED ME DOWN AGAIN LAST NIGHT.

SUZANNE? SHE'S HARMLESS. TELL HER TO CALL ME DIRECTLY IF SHE'S GOT A QUESTION OR A--

SHE ASKED ABOUT *THE WHITE BOX.*

what?

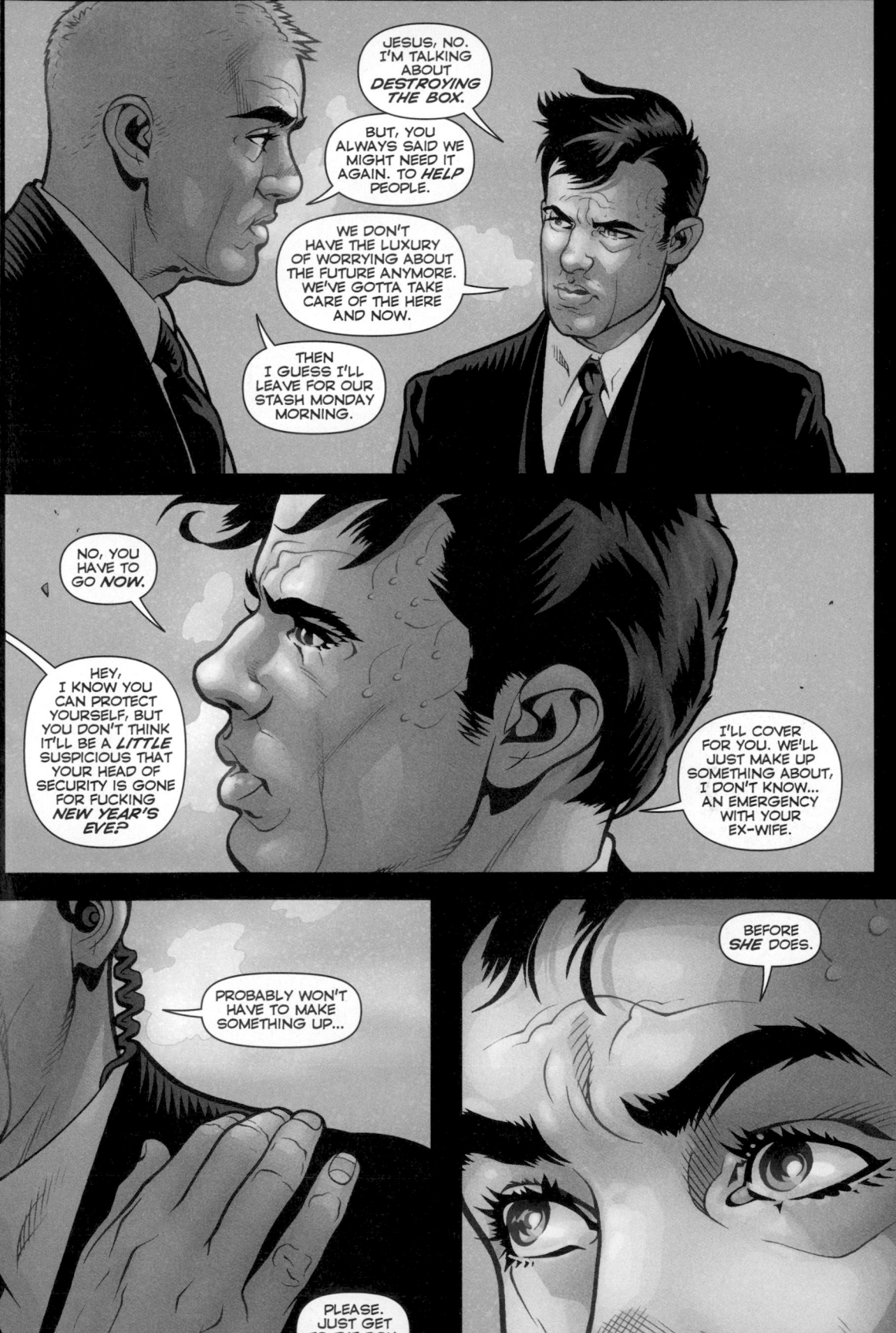

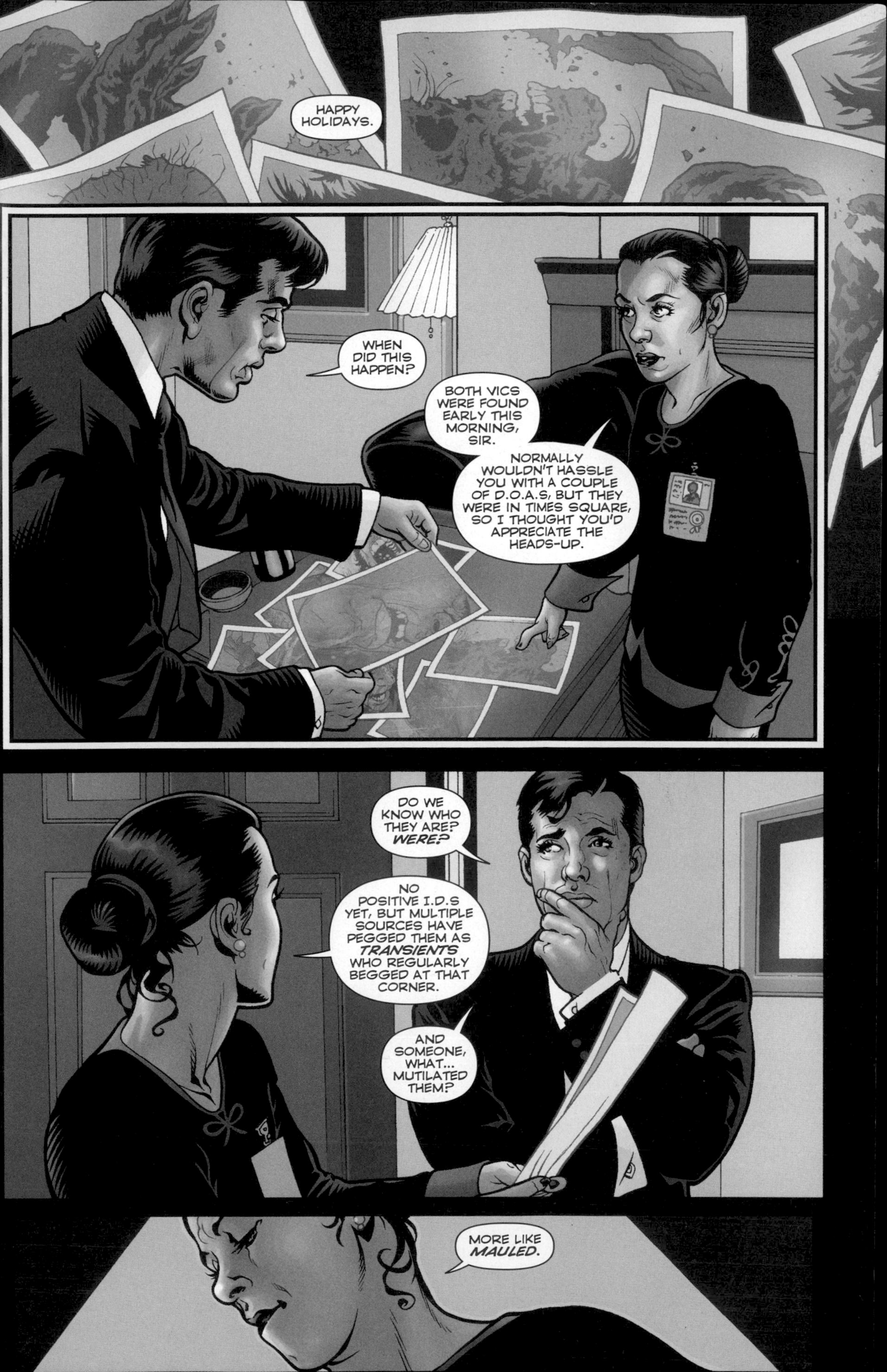

HAPPY HOLIDAYS.

WHEN DID THIS HAPPEN?

BOTH VICS WERE FOUND EARLY THIS MORNING, SIR.

NORMALLY WOULDN'T HASSLE YOU WITH A COUPLE OF D.O.A.S, BUT THEY WERE IN TIMES SQUARE, SO I THOUGHT YOU'D APPRECIATE THE HEADS-UP.

DO WE KNOW WHO THEY ARE? *WERE?*

NO POSITIVE I.D.S YET, BUT MULTIPLE SOURCES HAVE PEGGED THEM AS *TRANSIENTS* WHO REGULARLY BEGGED AT THAT CORNER.

AND SOMEONE, WHAT... MUTILATED THEM?

MORE LIKE *MAULED.*

Ring Out the Old
part 3

Chapter 5

FRIDAY, JUNE 1, 2001

YOU WANT TO UNDERSTAND WHAT MAKES EVERY-THING IN THIS WORLD TICK...EXCEPT *YOURSELF*.

THAT'S WHAT THEY CALL A *FATAL FLAW*.

WHAT THE FUCK DO *YOU* KNOW ABOUT FATAL, YOU UNDEAD PIECE OF SHIT?

YOU DON'T HAVE A CLUE ABOUT THE COLORS, DO YOU? ABOUT THE *SPECTRUM?*

YOU DON'T KNOW WHO YOU'RE REALLY SUPPOSED TO *BE*.

ARK ARK ARK

I...I NEVER HAD A DOG.

MY DAD SAID NEW YORK WAS NO PLACE TO RAISE AN ANIMAL.

I NEVER FORGAVE HIM FOR THAT.

I'M SORRY.

MITCH?

WHAT?! THIS HELMET IS SYMBOL OF... OF JUSTICE!

YEAH, WELL, TELL THAT TO THE POOR BASTARD I SUMMARILY *EXECUTED.*

DON'T BE DENSE, MITCHELL. PHERSON EXECUTED *HIMSELF.*

BESIDES, NO MATTER WHAT THIS ONE SAYS, WE DO NOT *KNOW* HE IS REALLY DEAD.

KREMLIN, YOU *SAW* THE PLACE THAT COCKLORD BLEW UP.

THERE WERE PARTS OF HIS BODY SCATTERED EVERYWHERE.

BUT NOT HIS *HEAD!*

GUYS, NONE OF THAT MATTERS ANYMORE.

ALL I KNOW IS... IT'S TIME FOR A CHANGE.

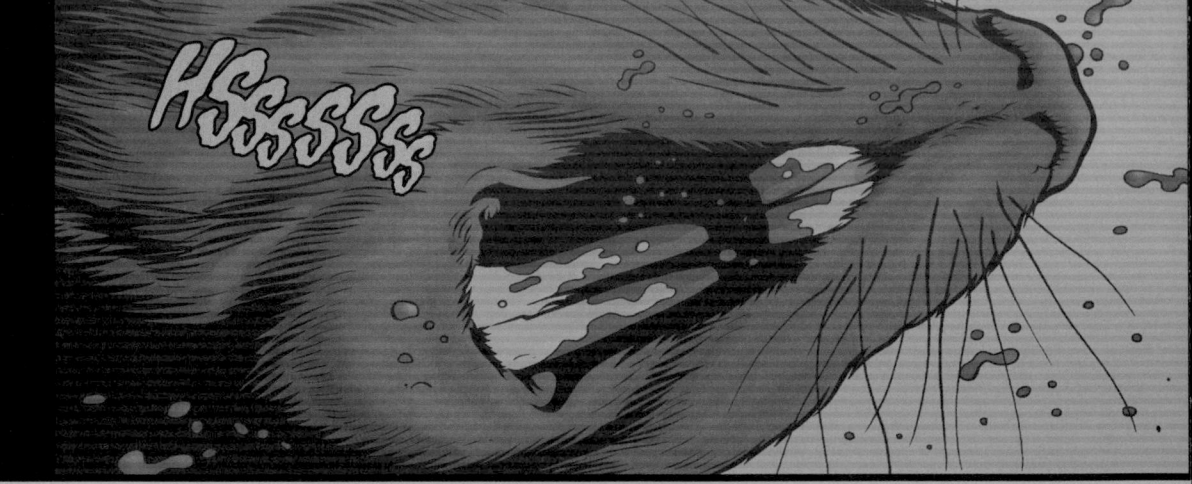

HSSSSSS

THURSDAY, DECEMBER 30, 2004

--AND IN BROOKLYN, ANOTHER MAN WAS *ATTACKED* WHILE LEAVING--

--*BITES* TO THE FACE LEFT A NINE-MONTH-OLD GIRL IN *CRITICAL CONDITION* AFTER--

--ARE *UNSURE* IF TONIGHT'S INCIDENTS HAVE ANY CONNECTION TO THE HOMELESS MAN AND WOMAN WHO WERE FOUND *DEAD* FROM APPARENT--

FUCK ME.

MAYOR HUNDRED?

SIR, THIS IS ALBERTO FINNEGAN, THE DEPARTMENT OF HEALTH'S LEAD EXTERMINATOR.

ACTUALLY, I PREFER "PEST CONTROLLER."

RATS CAN BE CONTAINED, BUT THEY'RE NEVER GONNA BE EXTERMINATED.

LET ME GUESS, EITHER WE PAY YOU TO FIX OUR PROBLEM OR YOU LURE ALL THE CHILDREN OUT OF TOWN WITH YOUR FLUTE.

SORRY...?

AH, I WAS HOPING MR. FINNEGAN COULD TELL US IF ANYTHING LIKE THIS EVER HAPPENED BEFORE.

WELL, HAVE YOU HEARD OF SOMETHING CALLED *MAUTAM?* HAPPENS IN INDIA EVERY FORTY-EIGHT YEARS. THEY'RE DUE FOR ANOTHER SOON.

I GUESS SOMETHING MAKES THE BAMBOO DIE, AND A PLAGUE OF *TWO MILLION RATS* SHOWS UP TO FEAST ON THE--

AL, HAS ANYTHING LIKE THIS EVER HAPPENED IN *NEW YORK CITY?*

TESTING, TESTING, ONE TWO THREE.

THIS IS ANGEL TWENTY-NINE CALLING HEAVEN.
I...I BELIEVE I CROSSED OVER.

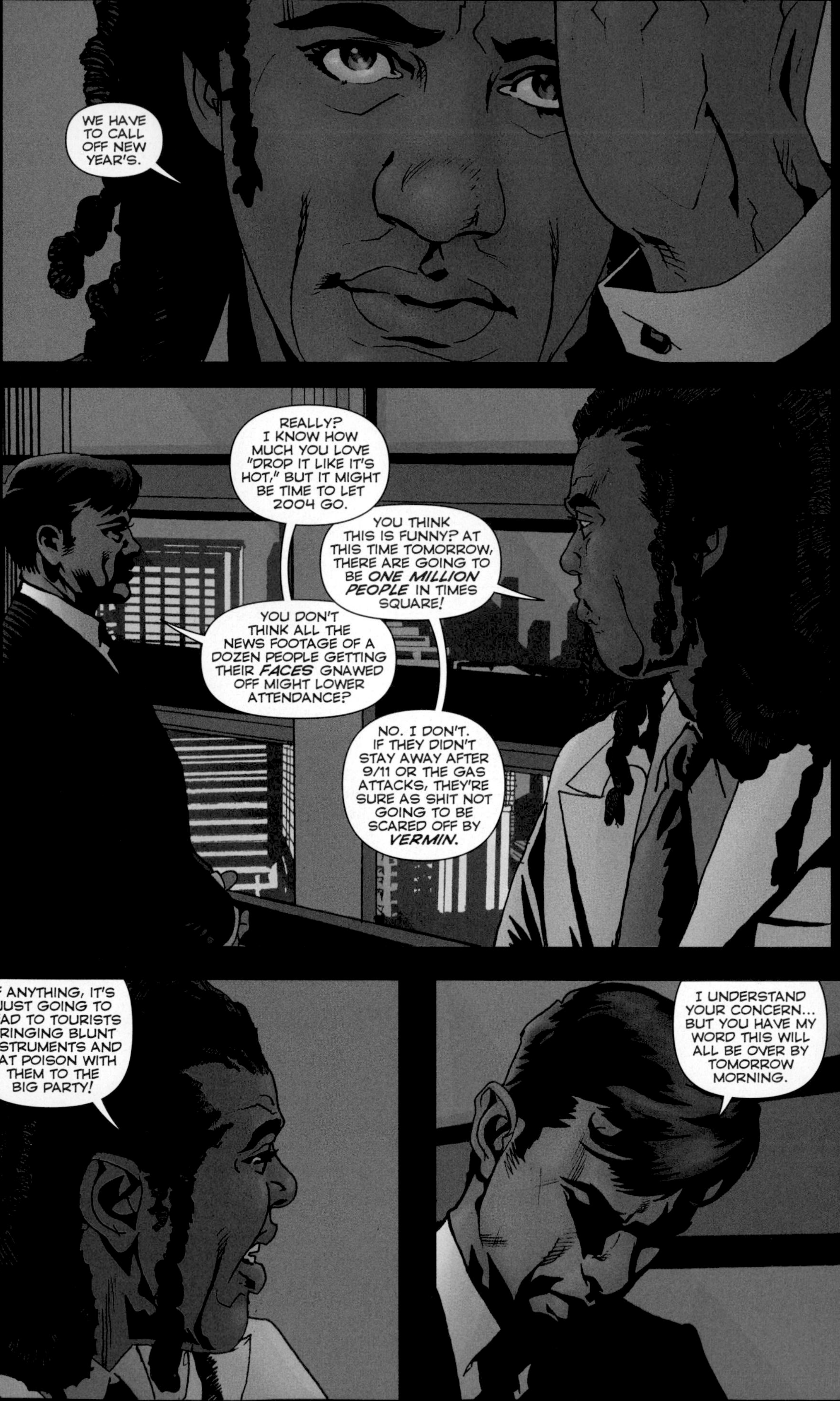

WE HAVE TO CALL OFF NEW YEAR'S.

REALLY? I KNOW HOW MUCH YOU LOVE "DROP IT LIKE IT'S HOT," BUT IT MIGHT BE TIME TO LET 2004 GO.

YOU THINK THIS IS FUNNY? AT THIS TIME TOMORROW, THERE ARE GOING TO BE *ONE MILLION PEOPLE* IN TIMES SQUARE!

YOU DON'T THINK ALL THE NEWS FOOTAGE OF A DOZEN PEOPLE GETTING THEIR *FACES* GNAWED OFF MIGHT LOWER ATTENDANCE?

NO. I DON'T. IF THEY DIDN'T STAY AWAY AFTER 9/11 OR THE GAS ATTACKS, THEY'RE SURE AS SHIT NOT GOING TO BE SCARED OFF BY *VERMIN.*

IF ANYTHING, IT'S JUST GOING TO LEAD TO TOURISTS BRINGING BLUNT INSTRUMENTS AND RAT POISON WITH THEM TO THE BIG PARTY!

I UNDERSTAND YOUR CONCERN... BUT YOU HAVE MY WORD THIS WILL ALL BE OVER BY TOMORROW MORNING.

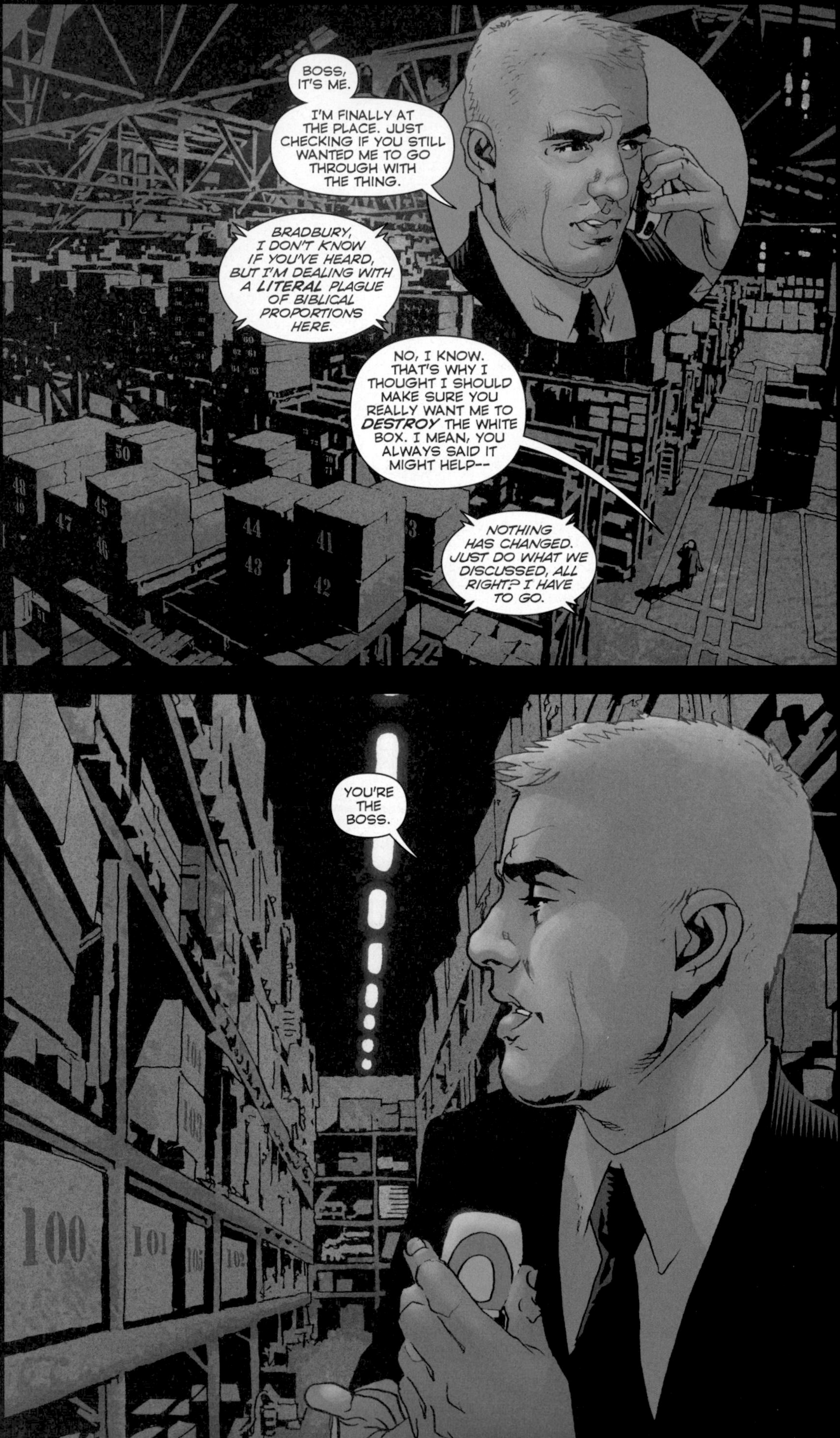

BOSS, IT'S ME.

I'M FINALLY AT THE PLACE. JUST CHECKING IF YOU STILL WANTED ME TO GO THROUGH WITH THE THING.

BRADBURY, I DON'T KNOW IF YOU'VE HEARD, BUT I'M DEALING WITH A *LITERAL* PLAGUE OF BIBLICAL PROPORTIONS HERE.

NO, I KNOW. THAT'S WHY I THOUGHT I SHOULD MAKE SURE YOU REALLY WANT ME TO *DESTROY* THE WHITE BOX. I MEAN, YOU ALWAYS SAID IT MIGHT HELP--

NOTHING HAS CHANGED. JUST DO WHAT WE DISCUSSED, ALL RIGHT? I HAVE TO GO.

YOU'RE THE BOSS.

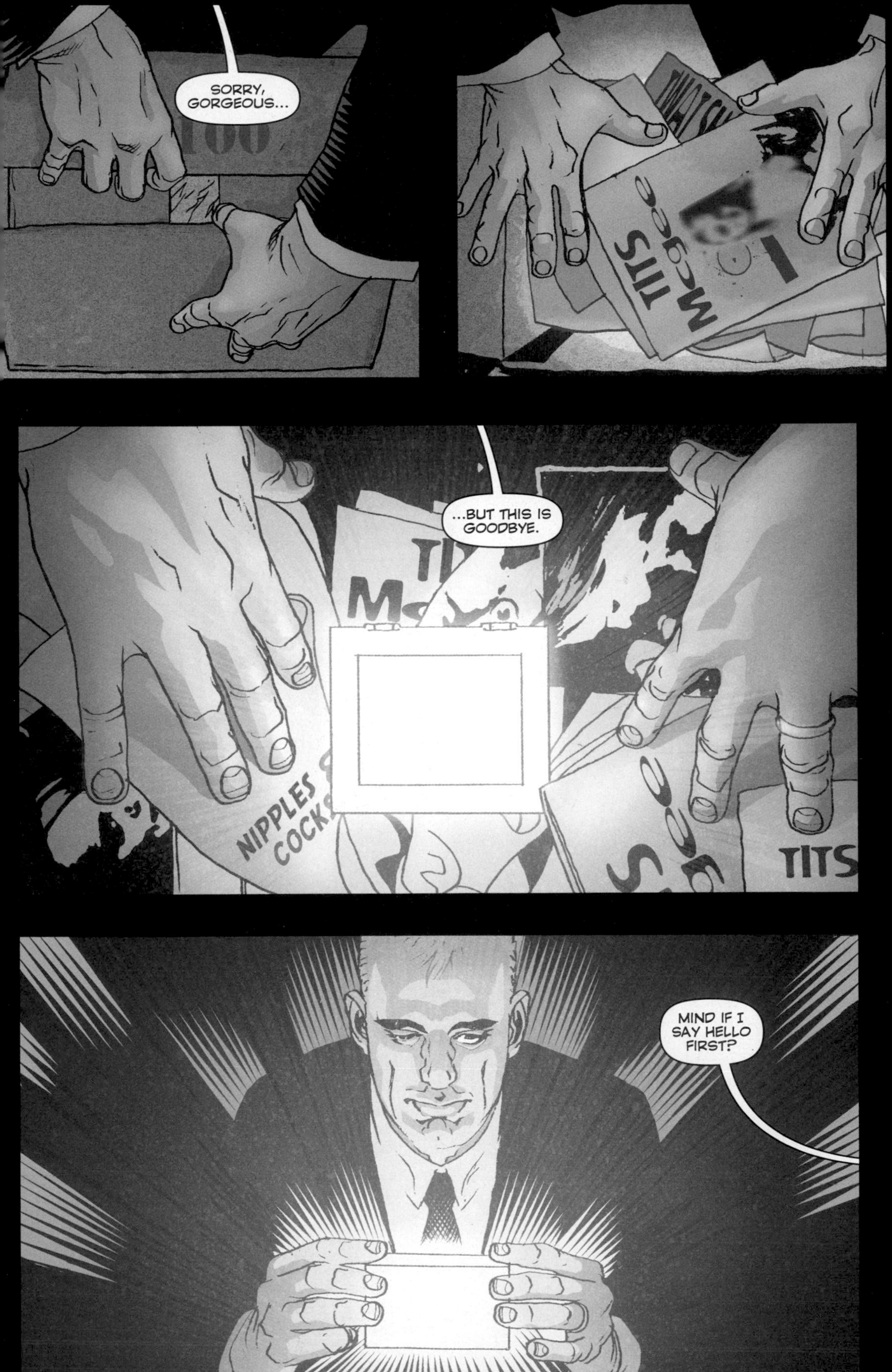

SORRY, GORGEOUS...

...BUT THIS IS GOODBYE.

MIND IF I SAY HELLO FIRST?

THE FUCK?!

REMEMBER ME?

YOU CAN STICK THAT PASS UP YOUR *HOLE*. THIS IS PRIVATE PROPERTY. I GOT EVERY RIGHT TO *END* YOU.

BESIDES, WHATEVER YOU THINK THIS IS ABOUT, I...I CAN GUARANTEE YOU YOU'RE *WRONG*.

PRESS
PRESS
ACCESS

THEN MAYBE YOU'D LIKE TO SET THE RECORD STRAIGHT?

JUST ONE QUESTION.

WHAT WERE YOU DOING WITH THE WHITE BOX ON THE MORNING OF NOVEMBER 6, 2001?

WHO?

TELL ME WHO *TOLD* YOU.

SORRY.

GONNA TAKE A LOT MORE THAN THAT FOR ME TO GIVE UP A SOURCE.

EVEN IF I SURVIVE, THIS IS PROBABLY THE *END* OF MY POLITICAL CAREER...BUT I REALIZE NOW I WAS STUPID TO EVER THINK I HAD A FUTURE BEYOND CITY HALL.

IT'S A LONG STORY, BUT THERE'S BEEN A NOOSE AROUND MY NECK SINCE THE DAY I WAS ELECTED, AND SOMEONE OUT THERE HAS FINALLY STARTED PULLING IT TAUT. SO MAYBE THIS IS FOR THE BEST.

ANYWAY, I'M *SORRY.* FOR... FOR EVERYTHING THAT'S HAPPENED TO US SINCE I TOOK OFFICE.

I THOUGHT YOU'D GET A KICK KNOWING I AT LEAST WENT OUT WEARING SOMETHING RIDICULOUS.

IT'S NOT YOUR FAVORITE, BUT JETPACKS AREN'T EXACTLY PRACTICAL UNDERGROUND.

COME TO THINK OF IT, I'M NOT SURE THE GODDAMN THINGS ARE PRACTICAL *ANYWHERE.*

RIGHT. WELL, TAKE CARE OF MY MOM, WILL YOU?

AND TELL BRADBURY I LOVED HIM.

Ring Out the Old
part 4

Chapter 6

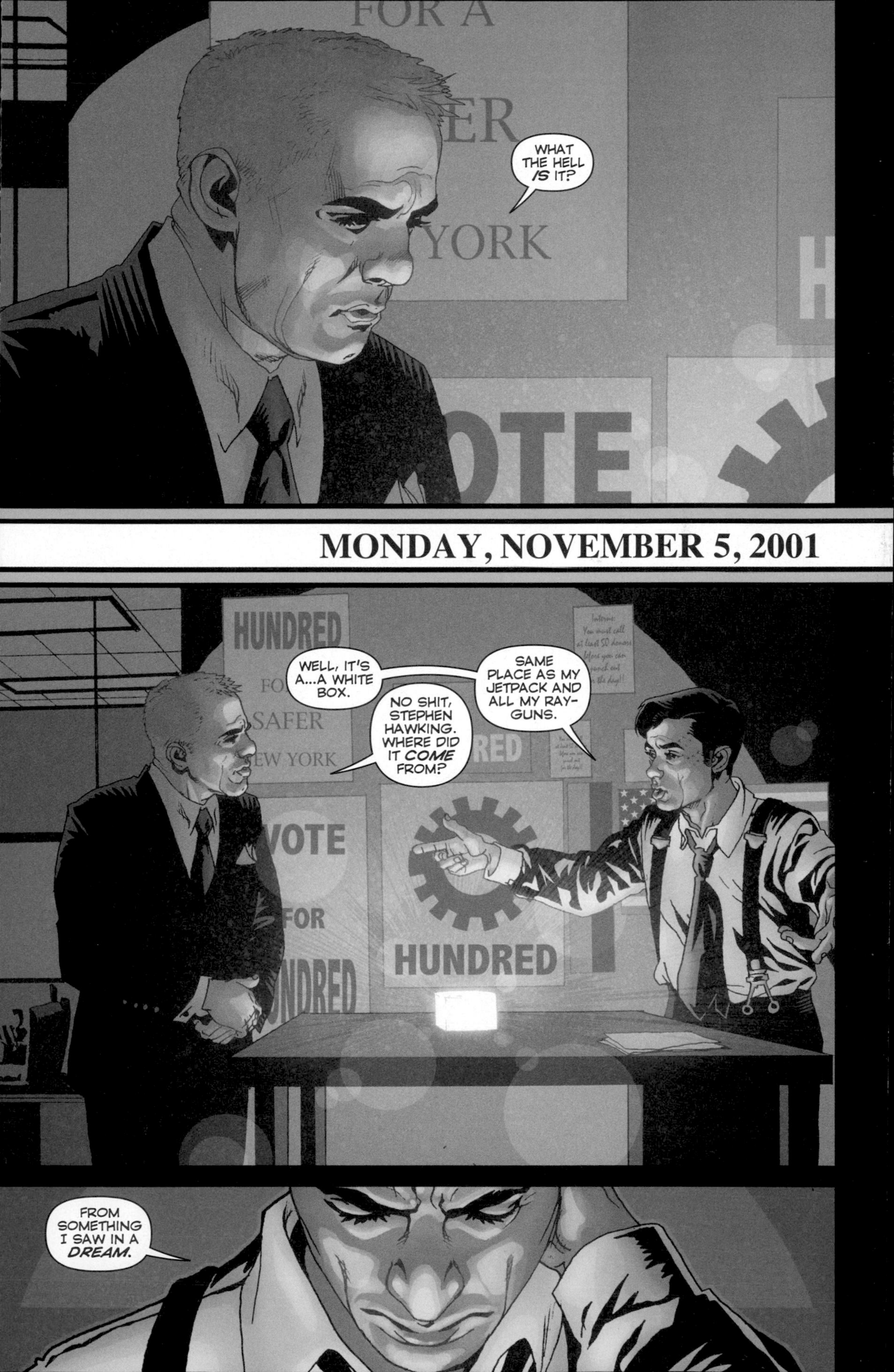

WHAT THE HELL *IS* IT?

MONDAY, NOVEMBER 5, 2001

WELL, IT'S A...A WHITE BOX.

NO SHIT, STEPHEN HAWKING. WHERE DID IT *COME* FROM?

SAME PLACE AS MY JETPACK AND ALL MY RAY-GUNS.

FROM SOMETHING I SAW IN A *DREAM.*

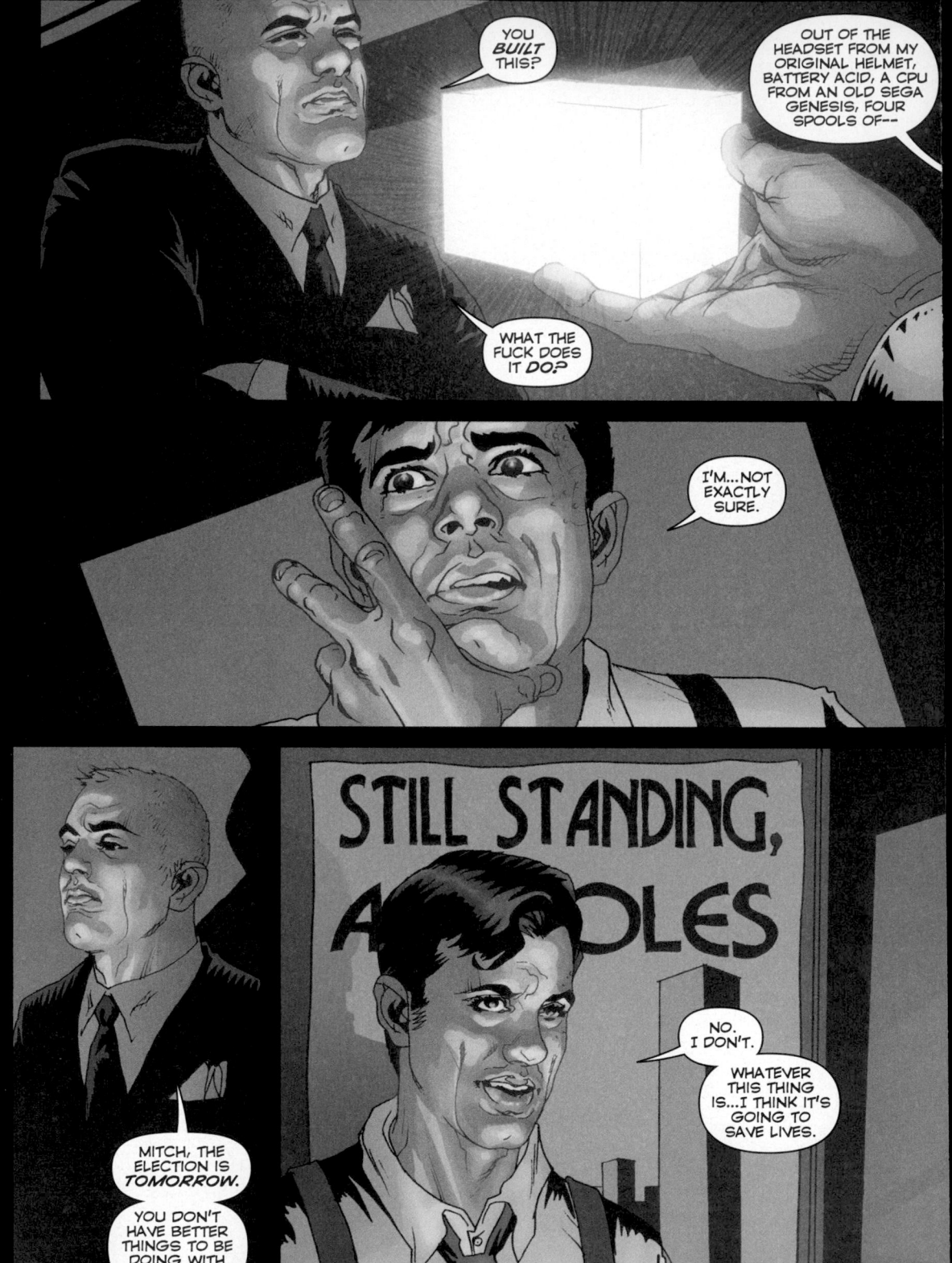

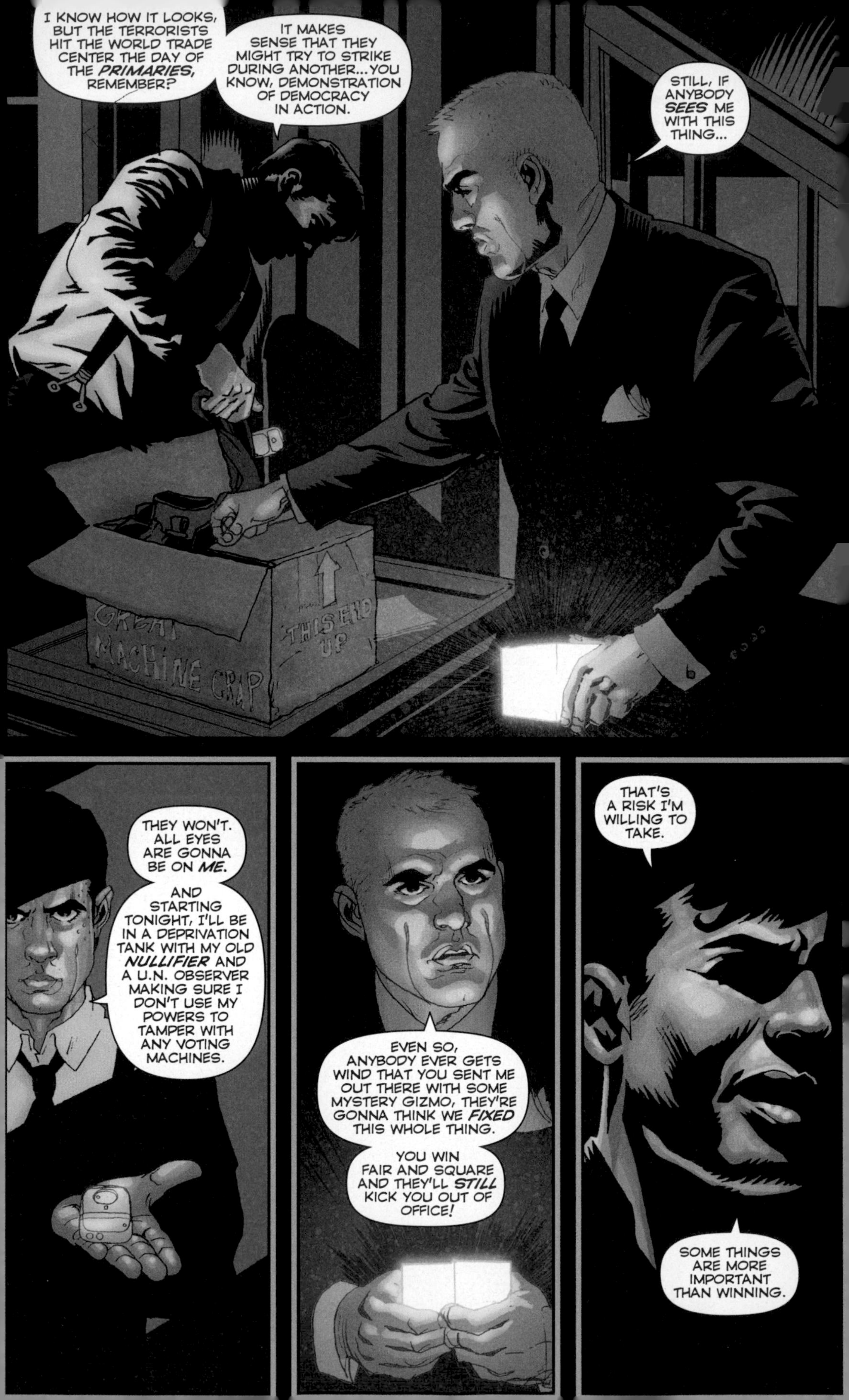

THURSDAY, DECEMBER 30, 2004

SKREEEE

SKREEEE

SKREEEE

CHRIST!

KZZZAKK

GET AWAY FROM ME!

LEAVE HIM BE, SMALL ONES.

HELLO, DEMON.

THEY *SAID* THE BLOOD WOULD BRING YOU TO ME.

WHAT THE AHHHHH!

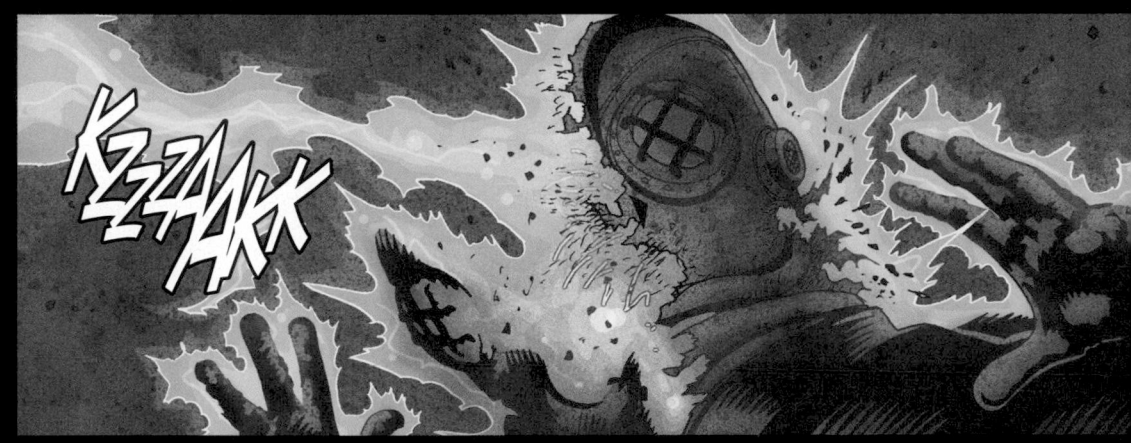

KZZZAAKK

I WAS SENT HERE TO TELL YOU THAT GOD IS VERY DISAPPOINTED.

YOU HAVE FORSAKEN THE TONGUES OF FIRE WITH WHICH YOU WERE BLESSED.

UM.

WHAT?

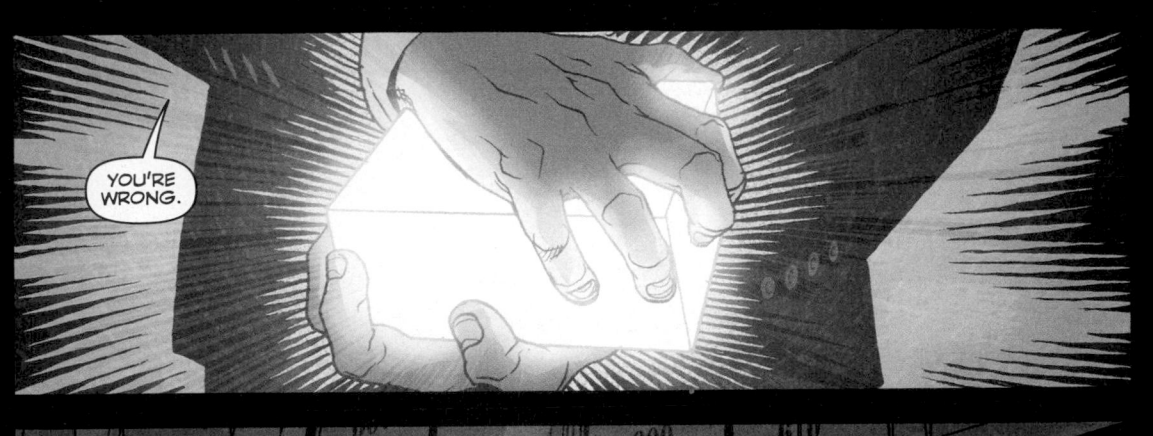

YOU'RE WRONG.

HUNDRED DIDN'T STEAL NOTHING. HE WON BY A GODDAMN LANDSLIDE!

HE WON BY 20,000 VOTES.

IT WAS ONLY CONSIDERED A LANDSLIDE BECAUSE OF HOW FAR BEHIND HE WAS IN THE POLLS AGAINST BOTH GREEN *AND* BLOOMBERG JUST THE DAY BEFORE.

WHATEVER, I GOT NOTHING TO SAY ON THE RECORD.

AND OFF THE RECORD?

I DON'T GIVE A SHIT IF HE RIGGED EVERY VOTE HE GOT.

HELL, IF THE ELECTION HAD BEEN ON 9/12, EVERY LAST NEW YORKER WOULD'VE PULLED THE LEVER FOR MITCH HUNDRED.
BUT IT WASN'T HELD THEN, BRADBURY. PEOPLE HAD ENOUGH DISTANCE TO THINK ABOUT HIS QUALIFICATIONS. HIS JUDGMENT. HIS BELIEFS.
YEAH, ENOUGH TIME FOR SOME DUMMIES TO FORGET THE SMELL OF JET FUEL AND BURNING BODIES.
GIVE THIS COUNTRY A HERO, AND THEY CAN'T WAIT TO TEAR HIM DOWN. I WASN'T GONNA LET THAT HAPPEN.
IF FOLKS WERE TOO STUPID TO RECOGNIZE THAT THE GUY WHO SAVED THAT TOWER WAS ALSO THE GUY WHO'D SAVE OUR CITY, THEN FUCK 'EM. FUCK THE WHOLE PROCESS.
IF YOU REALLY WANT TO KEEP US SAFE, YOU'LL GIVE THE WHITE BOX TO ME.
YOU'VE BEEN CARRYING THIS GUILT FOR SO LONG. PLEASE. JUST LET GO, AND I PROMISE--
THUK
NO!!

OH.
OH, JESUS.
SUZANNE? I'M SO SORRY. I DIDN'T MEAN...
ARE YOU...?
HURT? NO. JUST...DIFFERENT. WHATEVER WAS INSIDE THAT BOX, IT'S...I THINK IT'S INSIDE ME NOW. SAYING EXACTLY WHAT IT WANTS ME TO DO.
AND NOW YOU'RE GOING TO DO EXACTLY WHAT I SAY.

IT'S ALL OVER.

FUCKING A. THE ASSHOLES THAT SHAT YOU OUT WANNA COME HERE, I SAY *BRING 'EM ON.* THEY'RE GETTING NO HELP FROM ME.

YOU MISUNDERSTAND. MY READINGS NOW SUGGEST THAT *ANOTHER* WAVE ON THE SPECTRUM HAS JUST COME TO THE FORE. YOUR SERVICE IS NO LONGER NEEDED.

I DON'T FOLLOW. WHAT ARE YOU--

SPACK

UHNF!

NNNN.

WOW.

THIS YEAR... SUCKED...

 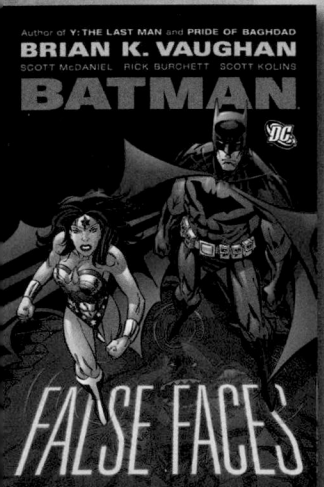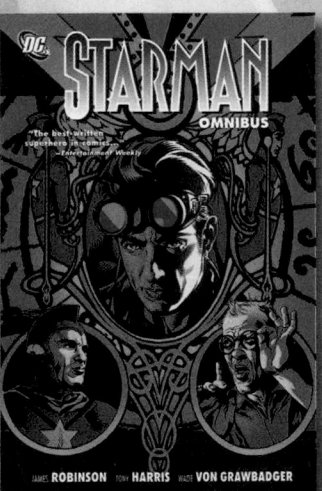

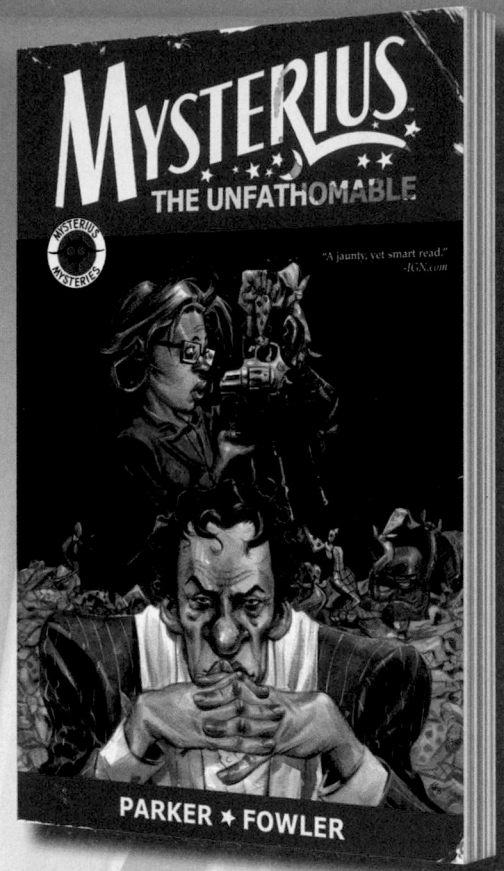

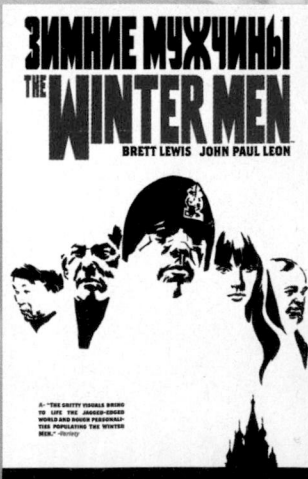